The Multinational Enterprise, EU Enlargement and Central Europe

Also by Yusaf H. Akbar

GLOBAL ANTITRUST: Trade and Competition Linkages

The Multinational Enterprise, EU Enlargement and Central Europe

The Effects of Regulatory Convergence

Yusaf H. Akbar

CERAM Graduate School of Management and Technology
Sophia-Antipolis
France

First published 2003 by
PALGRAVE MACMILLAN
Houndmills, Basingstoke, Hampshire RG21 6XS and
175 Fifth Avenue, New York, N.Y. 10010
Companies and representatives throughout the world

PALGRAVE MACMILLAN is the global academic imprint of the Palgrave Macmillan division of St. Martin's Press, LLC and of Palgrave Macmillan Ltd. Macmillan® is a registered trademark in the United States, United Kingdom and other countries. Palgrave is a registered trademark in the European Union and other countries.

ISBN 0–333–91988–2

This book is printed on paper suitable for recycling and made from fully managed and sustained forest sources.

A catalogue record for this book is available from the British Library.

Library of Congress Cataloging-in-Publication Data
Akbar, Yusaf H., 1969–
The multinational enterprise, EU enlargement and Central Europe: the effects of regulatory convergence / Yusaf H. Akbar.
    p.   cm.
Includes bibliographical references and index.
ISBN 0–333–91988–2 (cloth)
1. International business enterprises—European Union countries—Management.   2. Industrial laws and legislation—European Union countries.   3. Europe—Economic integration.   4. European Union—Hungary.   I. Title: Multinational enterprise, European Union enlargement and Central Europe.   II. Title.
HD62.4 .A38 2002
338.8'884—dc21

200208749

10   9   8   7   6   5   4   3   2   1
12   11   10   09   08   07   06   05   04   03

Printed and bound in Great Britain by
Antony Rowe Ltd, Chippenham and Eastbourne

Contents

List of Tables and Figures

Tables

Figures

Preface

I use not only all the brains I have, but all I can borrow
Woodrow Wilson

This book is the result of an interest in the process of change in East
and Central Europe that was kindled as both an undergraduate and
then a doctoral student at the University of Sussex. As part of that
learning process at Sussex, and for my MA degree at the College of
Europe, I also became intensely fascinated in explaining the new
political landscape developing both in Europe and the wider world.
The increasing role of the multinational enterprise in the political
and policy-making landscape in the world political economy has
become increasingly evident to scholars. This book aims to contribute to this research. By focusing on the process of EU enlargement,
I have tried to bring together a crucial issue for the future of Europe
and also to examine the political role of the multinational enterprise.
Hungary is undergoing a remarkable process of internationalization
that has brought it to the threshold of the European Union. It has
provided an excellent case study for my research.

I would like to thank a number of people and organizations for
help and support in the financial, intellectual and spiritual field. First,
I would like to thank Professor Eric de la Croix, former Academic Director
of the European Business School, London, for his support in allowing
me to take a sabbatical. I would also like to thank Professor Paul
Marer, Academic Director at IMC Graduate School of Management,
for being flexible about my teaching schedule and lobbying for financial support for research. Thanks also go to Dr J. Brad McBride who
has worked with me on the issues in the Hungarian banking sector.
Organizations that were pivotal in enabling this research include the
Civic Education Project, IMC Graduate School of Management, Central
European University and the Institute for Social and European Studies,
all in Budapest. I would like to thank my research assistants Katalin
Csiky, Agnes Kozma and Borbala Toth who helped at various stages

in translation, interviews and data collection. Last, but not least, I would like to thank my father, Susan and Zarina, my sisters, for being my flesh and blood and supporting me spiritually during the many difficult moments of living in Hungary.

1
Introduction

1.1 Introduction

In enlarging the European Union (EU) to include thirteen new states,[1] the EU and its member states have agreed to undertake the largest and most challenging process of regulatory and legal convergence to date in the history of the EU. While the average economic size of the enlargement countries in terms of GDP and population is not as great as the current EU average, the nature of the political economies that will form part of the enlarged EU are unique for several reasons. First, with the exception of Cyprus, Malta and Turkey, all these political economies have undergone significant transition and transformation since 1989 when the state socialist economies collapsed. The reasons for the collapse are now well-documented. Indeed our study does not seek to reanalyse these events. Second, the new states applying will be faced with the most sophisticated and detailed set of supranational rules formulated to date in the EU. It is interesting to note that the level of EU legislation currently required to be implemented by the new states dwarfs the level faced by Spain and Portugal in 1986 and the 1995 states (Sweden, Finland and Austria). Moreover, in the latter case, the regulatory capacity of these states was considerably higher than the transforming economies of East and Central Europe (ECE) who are currently seeking membership.

Thus the combination of low levels of administrative resources and the unprecedented amount of new laws and regulations to be implemented and enforced imply that the current process will be long and costly. Thus from the point of view of administrative and state political governance, we should expect a unique enlargement.

Crucial to our arguments laid out in this book is the realization that while states remain, and will continue to remain, the central driving force behind the successful enlargement of the EU, we need to reconsider and redefine the political economy of regulation under which this current process will occur. This is because an array of non-state actors will be and currently are involved in the process of influencing, framing and formulating positions on the myriad issues of regulation and the necessary convergence. Put more directly, we cannot simply assume that the business of enlargement is conducted wholly by representatives of nation-states. Rather the picture that we seek to paint is one of complex, multilevel interactions between states, firms, non-governmental organizations (NGOs) and EU institutions. Those familiar with the EU integration literature will not be surprised by this claim. There is a rich literature on this issue (e.g. Green Cowles 1997; Cawson 1995, 1997; Wallace and Young 1997; Majone 1990). However, both the IPE and more generally international relations literature is somewhat more divided on the state and non-state actors debate. For example, Andrew Moravscik (1998), one of the most important scholars in the field of European integration, claims that EU politics is merely an extension of domestic politics and in particular of the policy aims of member states. Where non-state actors interface in this process is therefore predominantly at the level of domestic politics.

By contrast, we highlight the work of Ernst Haas (1964) that emphasized the role of supranational institutions and policy spillover for the causes of European integration. Rosamond (2000) refers to this as a debate between the 'Harvard' and 'Stanford' schools. Implicitly in their work, there is a role for non-state actors but once again their focus remains on the state and the international governmental organization (IGO), in this case, the EU Commission and other institutions.

In order for us to do this, we need to reformulate our 'map' of the global political economy (GPE), the actors who play influential and determining roles and the balance of 'power' between these actors. In doing so, this book aims to build on existing literature on redefining the GPE, and the discipline devoted to studying it.[2]

While the broad theoretical aim of the book is to develop our conceptualization of the international politics of the firm, the empirical project is an analysis of the regulatory challenges facing both the current EU and in particular the candidate countries. More specifically this book focuses on regulatory convergence, which is the process through which candidate countries adopt existing EU rules in order to complete the necessary stages for membership.

Traditionally, the question of regulatory convergence has been analysed with a focus on states (e.g. Wallace and Young 1997; Middlemas 1997). To date, there has been a relative paucity of work that looks at the role of firms. This book is a project that tackles three main questions. First, what is the role of the multinational enterprise (MNE) as a non-state actor in our conceptualizations of international political economy (IPE)? Second, how does the business strategy literature help us contribute to understanding the process of regulatory convergence? Third, and more specifically, how do business strategies of the MNE facilitate regulatory convergence in the EU accession states in East and Central Europe (ECE)?

In many senses, our book is somewhat different from the current literature in that it tackles an issue covered in the EU regulatory convergence literature that hitherto has focused predominantly on the role of states in this process. Where firms have been specifically analysed, it has been in their role as lobbyists (Coen 1997; Coen and Grant 2000; Wallace and Young 1997). Even then, they have been conceptualized as 'influencers' and therefore the focus has still been on the state and the impact of firms is therefore considered as a secondary effect.

On the other hand, this book is influenced by the literature on the role of firms as political actors pioneered by Susan Strange and John Stopford (Stopford and Strange 1991). This literature asserts that we need to reconsider the nature of international diplomacy that has traditionally focused on inter-state relations. This is because there has been a fundamental change in the nature of economic wealth creation in two ways. First, the role of the state as wealth creator has been reduced. This is due in large part to the apparent failure of the state to solve economic crises in the 1970s. Second, the role of the MNE and its international or transnational reach has meant that wealth creation occurs outside of traditionally accepted democratic (or at least accountable) institutions[3] and that it is created increasingly in a transnational way through MNE production.

As Cerny (1995) and Palan and Abbot (1998) assert, this implies that the role of the state has shifted from a redistributive, welfare state towards a 'competition' state as states compete with each other to capture the benefits of wealth creation brought by the MNE.

In turn, this implies the need for states to bargain with firms in a less traditional but similar fashion to inter-state diplomacy. When the role of MNE alliances, i.e. firm–firm diplomacy is included, Stopford and Strange (1991) argue that a new diplomatic 'triangle' emerges which is an important and arguably far-reaching reconceptualization of the international system. Certainly it implies that the world of economic diplomacy is considerably richer than has been traditionally considered in the IPE literature hitherto.

Given the important contribution of this literature, this book aims to draw two further literatures into the debate. First is the international business literature pioneered by Michael Porter's (1990) competitive strategy 'trilogy'. The aim of this work was to move beyond theoretical economic explanations for industrial organization and trade and provide a framework for international business strategy literature that had hitherto lacked rigour and was arguably somewhat anecdotal and taxonomic in its approach. Porter, and those who followed, developed direct strategic and policy-related implications from their work. Indeed, Michael Porter has in many senses cornered a position in the market for strategic management studies by using theory to develop general strategic frameworks for companies. This literature is useful in this study in that it creates a method through which the firm is no longer considered a 'black box' as in the industrial organization literature, which has largely concerned itself with market structure and performance. Once we can directly 'model' firm strategy, we can apply this to the impact of this strategy on regulatory convergence.

In order to understand why, it is necessary to bring in a fourth literature. Economists and political scientists have also been active in the generation of research on the formulation of 'optimal' regulatory regimes. This normative policy work has sought largely to critique existing regulatory frameworks in a range of contexts (e.g. the shift from national to supranational policy governance; public policy reforms such as privatization) and offered suggestions for policy development or reform. As is the current intellectual vogue, a significant degree of this literature has focused on the increasing salience of economic efficiency in both static and dynamic contexts and how a shift towards market-based governance can enhance the regulatory framework to benefit producers and consumers. Thus this literature implicitly enhances the role of market operators in the creation and functioning of regulatory systems.

For the purposes of our book, this approach lends an insight into the thinking behind public policy-makers and how the private sector can influence their policy proposals. It also allows us to develop a direct relationship between firm strategy and the degree of regulatory convergence. This is because if firm strategy, which inevitably shapes market structure and performance, is largely an empirical yardstick through which policy-makers develop policy, then as firms' strategic behaviour generates 'best practice', this will force regulatory regimes to reflect this.

These diverse literatures, in attempting to bring in specific issues in some detail, clearly expand our knowledge and understanding of the GPE and the role firms play in it.

1.2 Methodological issues

Our book is an attempt to combine robust theoretical propositions with rich empirical material. We believe that this approach and understanding of the dynamics of regulatory convergence is likely to be increasingly important in the future as the liberalization of the world economy will force states to adopt an increasing scope and depth of multilateral agreements. Examples of this are the increasing co-operation and global rule-making under the World Trade Organization (WTO) in the areas of intellectual property rights (IPRs), trade-related investment measures (TRIMs) and competition policy.

This inevitably implies that as the pressures for regulatory convergence increase, the resources required by states to meet the terms of convergence will need to increase commensurately. This is combined with the increasingly clear evidence of the technocratic role of the MNE in influencing multilateral regulatory frameworks. Thus the influence of corporate strategy in influencing the process of regulatory convergence is likely to be increasingly important. Current moves towards creating a free-trade area spanning the Americas, deepening integration in Mercosur and negotiations to create a transatlantic free-trade area all suggest that this issue will become more important in the future.

Once the conceptual framework is set out, the next stage is to develop a credible empirical methodology. There are a number of methodological issues at play here. We have chosen Hungary as the country case study for our research. This is because Hungary has been the largest per capita recipient of FDI in the ECE region until 2001 and therefore the role of FDI on regulatory convergence is likely to be significant. More than 50 per cent of Hungarian GDP is produced by foreign companies; over three-quarters of Hungary's total exports are produced by MNEs based in Hungary.

Second, we have chosen one type of FDI: the market serving type. This is because, as we explain in detail in Chapter 5, the impact of MNE strategy on regulatory convergence is likely to be significantly identifiable, as the main strategic objective of this FDI is to supply services or goods to the local market. In this sense, we believe that MNEs use higher standards as a tool of competitive rivalry with local companies. This should, *ceteris paribus*, facilitate the process of regulatory convergence as we argue in Chapter 4 which outlines our principal conceptual framework.

As the effect that the study seeks to highlight in this book is an indirect one, the means that are used to evaluate the importance of this effect cannot necessarily be derived solely by reference to measured and published data. Rather, the study relies upon inference from a range of sources. These include in-depth interviews with relevant actors and reports from governmental, business and non-governmental sectors. This issue is dealt with in some detail in Chapter 5.

1.3 The case studies: market serving FDI

We have chosen three industries as case studies for our research. These are the banking, telecommunications and electricity sectors respectively. These have been chosen as they have all been subject to substantial strategic FDI from MNEs from the EU and the USA. We should thus expect that these sectors are where the FDI effect on regulatory convergence should be highest. Second, these sectors, in the EU, are subject to EU-wide liberalization and regulatory regimes that require substantial changes in Hungarian domestic legislation and regulations in order for these sectors to be compliant with the *acquis*. Thus the regulatory convergence challenge is significant in these sectors. Third, we can examine how the degree of competition in a given sector will affect the degree of regulatory convergence caused by the role of FDI.

It should be expected that as the level of actual or potential competition between MNEs and with local companies increases, the pressure to use higher standards as part of their competitive strategy should increase.

Fourth, as part of a broader discussion on the role of MNEs in economic development, we have selected these three cases as they are industries that are fundamental to the successful functioning of other sectors in the economy. Successful liberalization of these sectors is likely to increase the productive potential and efficiency of these sectors through the spillover impact this will have for the rest of the Hungarian political economy. While we do not claim to be offering a study that endorses FDI as central to an economic development strategy for transition and developing economies, it is interesting to examine how FDI has affected the economic infrastructure of the Hungarian political economy.

1.4 Structure of the book

Our study is organized as follows. In Chapter 2, we review the literature on the MNE, the theory of international production and the IPE of the MNE and its relationship with states and regulatory systems. We draw attention to the difference between FDI for resource-seeking and market-serving purposes. In this chapter we also examine how the interdisciplinary field of European Studies, largely in response to the empirical reality of EU integration, has developed concepts to understand the relationship between states and MNEs. In Chapter 3, we set out in detail the empirical setting of our research: the process of economic and political transition in ECE political economies and the project of EU enlargement to incorporate these states. In this chapter we include an in-depth narrative of the developing EU–ECE political and economic relationship. We also have an in-depth analysis of FDI trends in Hungary.

In Chapter 4, we offer our conceptual framework on the relationship between competitive advantage and regulatory convergence. We develop some models and scenarios of how FDI can affect regulatory convergence. Chapter 5 tackles methodological issues in preparation for our case studies. In this chapter we consider the empirical challenge of assessing the link between FDI and regulatory convergence; we outline the questionnaire method used in our case studies and we offer some preliminary hypotheses on what we expect to find from our case studies.

Chapters 6 through 8 are case study chapters examining the banking, electricity and telecommunications sectors respectively. Each chapter includes a detailed narrative on the development of the sector after 1989. We also provide a detailed industry analysis and in particular focus on ownership of the sectors concerned. Each chapter also has a section on the EU legislation relevant to each sector. Lastly each chapter includes a detailed analysis of the relationship between FDI and regulatory convergence basing our insights on our primary and secondary research material.

In Chapter 6, the banking sector is examined. We find that the role of foreign banks was substantial in the implementation of EU-compliant legislation as early as 1998. Problems of domestic personal lending and the mortgage market aside, foreign banks have used their competitive advantage in supplying EU-compliant banking services to MNEs based in Hungary. This competitive threat has forced Hungary's largest retail bank, OTP Bank, to significantly improve its own operations and services offered to Hungarian retail customers. This case is the strongest evidence of the role played by MNEs in promoting regulatory convergence towards EU standards.

The evidence from Chapter 7 is not as strong as in the banking sector. While demonstrating the positive role of MNE ownership of Hungarian electricity generation and distribution companies in promoting regulatory convergence, the nature of industrial structure, being essentially characterized as a natural network monopoly, means that an absence of competition at the start of the privatization process has held back the degree to which MNEs have been required to use higher regulatory standards to compete. German, North American, French and Belgian companies dominate ownership of the distribution and generation sides of the sector. The monopoly contracts granted to the companies partially resulted in the slower pace of introduction of EU-compliant legislation. In 2001, the liberalization process has allowed for competition for supply of customers using more than 100 mW. This is the first step in the full introduction of the EU Electricity Directive.

Our last case study examines the telecommunications sector. Foreign ownership in the various sub-sectors of the telecommunications industry is pervasive with the role of Deutsche Telekom, through ownership of MATÁV, the national and long-distance fixed-line supplier, and Westel, Hungary's largest mobile telephone services company, being particularly important. Vivendi of France is also an important player in the Hungarian sector and is largely regarded as the major competitor to Deutsche Telekom given the implementation of the EU-compliant Communications Act that came into effect in December 2001.

Chapter 9 is our concluding chapter in which we summarize our findings in each sector and then discuss the applicability of our research to other regions of the world political economy. We also consider the shortcomings and limitations of the research as well as a future research agenda for this type of analysis. Lastly, we also examine the emerging synthesis of IB and IPE literatures.

2
Setting the Scene

2.1 Introduction

Why do MNEs exist? What structural changes in the world political economy have encouraged the development of MNEs? How do the disciplines of IPE and IBS understand the role of MNEs? We shall address these central questions in this chapter. The reason for undertaking an analysis of these questions is in order to provide an analytical framework for our research. Underlying this is an attempt to build on an emerging synthesis between IPE and IBS on the nature of the relationship between governmental and private authority in the international system. We argue that the work of a number of scholars in both fields (Strange 1988a, 1988b, 1996 and Vernon 1966, 1971, 1979, 1993 in IPE, and Cantwell 1991, Casson 1985, 1987, Dunning 1988a, 1988b, Porter 1980, 1990 and Rugman and Verbeke 1990 in IBS) has provided crucial theoretical and conceptual frameworks in which we and other scholars are seeking to build (e.g. Baron 1995, 1997; Cawson 1997; Coen 1997; Coen and Grant 2000; Cowles 1997; Cutler et al. 1999; Hocking and McGuire 2001; Milner 1988; Maxwell et al. 1997; Yoffie 1993).

The chapter is organized as follows. Part one considers how IPE and IBS as disciplines conceptualize the relationship between states and MNEs. Part two is a detailed evaluation of the main theoretical contributions to the understanding of MNEs in the IPE and IBS literature. Part three provides a conceptual basis for the synthesis of IPE and IBS approaches. This section links to Chapter 3, which is the key methodological chapter that outlines our theoretical approach linking

MNE activity to the process of regulatory convergence between differing systems of economic regulation between states.

2.2 The relationship between IPE and IBS

The two disciplines of IPE and IBS have much in common. IPE focuses predominantly on how the state affects the allocation, elaboration and distribution of economic resources in the marketplace, whereas the IBS literature examines the positive strategic and operational questions facing an MNE. Eden and Potter (1993: 34) argue that, consequently, the IBS literature has tended to de-emphasize a critical discussion of the normative impact of MNEs on society. Put another way, IBS has 'de-politicized' the activities of the MNE. By contrast, the IPE literature has taken a stronger normative position of the role of the market and market actors. Moreover, IPE as a much broader constituency of analysis than IBS has several contending views of the MNE. It is possible to consider three broad schools. These are the realist, liberal and critical approaches.

Realists in IPE consider the role of states as supreme in the world political economy (e.g. Gilpin 1975; Spero 1990). The realists identify the MNE as a threat to the power of states and thereby implicitly posit an antagonistic relationship between state power and MNE power. The normative implication of this school is that MNEs should be regulated by the state and where necessary in multilateral, inter-governmental forums to preserve state sovereignty over economic, political and security resources. This view is sometimes considered as neo-mercantilist and nationalist and within a broad brush of historical analysis is frequently identified with attempts by LDCs to renationalize assets owned by MNEs in the 1950s and 1960s.

The liberal school, while divided on the normative benefits of the MNE (e.g. Frieden and Lake 1987; Strange 1988a), recognizes that it is a force for integration in the world political economy. Some argue that MNEs should be regarded as positive agents for change as in the past half-century MNEs have shifted economic resources and technology to a broader range of societies and political economies. Others claim that a direct impact of the multinationalization of production has been an increased inequality of wealth between skilled and unskilled individuals and between resource-rich and resource-poor countries. The most current phase of transformation in the world political economy, where technology has become a central driver of change, has exposed these effects of MNE activity. The policy implication of the liberal analysis is that MNE activity needs to be regulated on a multi-lateral level where the impact of MNE behaviour has a manifestly negative impact on society. Moreover, states should cooperate to ensure that adequate compensation and adjustment mechanisms are in place to enable societies to develop in response to this irreversible shift of economic activity.

The critical school tends to place the MNE as an actor within a broader, neo-Marxist or neo-Gramscian critique of capitalism as a structural organization of the world political economy (e.g. Gill and Law 1988; Prebisch 1970; Wallerstein 1989; Palan and Abbot 1998). Scholars in this school argue that MNEs are a manifestation of the exploitative nature of global capitalism. They systematically exploit and promote underdevelopment in the periphery and semi-periphery of the world political economy. MNEs represent a form of neo-colonialism, as they act at the behest of their home governments and collaborate with elites in host countries. This view gained significant currency in the work of the *dependencia* scholars such as Raul Prebisch who examined the impact of economic liberalization in Latin America in the 1960s. More broadly, the work of the United Nations Council on Trade and Development (UNCTAD) in the 1960s and 1970s reflected this critical view. The normative implication of the critical school is that global capitalism needs to be fundamentally reformed (if not abolished). Interestingly, we can see similar normative claims from the realist and critical schools: both suggest controls and restraints on the activities of MNEs. The main difference, of course, is that realists only consider the threat to states caused by transnational activity whereas the critical scholars identify a more fundamental critique of capitalism as the reason for change.

While there are quite radical differences between these three schools, they share a common perspective: the state–market relationship. The contention, often forwarded in the IPE literature, that states are in a complex relationship with the marketplace (Strange 1988a) arguably confuses the structural-agency relationship between an MNE and the state. In most concepts of IPE (and international relations more generally), the state is an actor in the international system. Firms are somewhat secondary or appended concepts in even IPE analysis.[1] The 'market' is rather a systemic or structural feature of politico-economic organization of the international system and thus we need to search within this structure for actors whose primary locus of activity is the marketplace. As we are interested in the trans- or international features of the structures of markets, the obvious actor to focus on is the MNE. This itself is a feature of the development of IPE from more traditional origins in political science and (to a lesser degree) economics (in its scientized form). Scholars in IPE are interested in states by virtue of their academic training in political science, their closer links to governmental authority and, arguably, a fundamental distaste for business studies as a bona fide discipline. Where IPE has developed systematic study of the nature of the MNE, the research has frequently been carried out by scholars who have experience in the private sector and based on close collaboration between IPE and IBS scholars.

This is where we argue the IBS literature could be extremely useful in moving away from the 'black box' depiction of the MNE. As our central contention in this book is that we need to build on an emerging synthesis of IBS and IPE literature to understand the relationship between the MNE as an a non-governmental authority on the one hand and states and international organizations (IOs) as governmental authority on the other, it is useful as a first proxy of this synthesis to consider the analytical insights of the IBS literature.

2.3 The IBS literature and the development of theory of international production

It is important to note that IBS as a discipline has suffered from the same 'disciplinary tunnel vision' as some aspects of IPE for two reasons. First, this is due to the origins of IBS as an academic discipline. Business studies as an academic subject has emerged as the least academic of scholarly disciplines. Based around the provision of professional training for future or current managers, the educational and technical background of business studies scholars has frequently been from operational areas of industry such as engineering, finance and marketing. One of the main criticisms levelled at business schools is that business research tends to lack theoretical rigour. Business scholars, of course, contend that this is an over-generalization and that research for business should have a strong applied and empirical content given the nature of the need for business education in serving industry rather than training future academics. This is reinforced by the fact that an important number of business scholars have considerable professional experience, and consequently are well connected with the business world.[2]

Second, an increasing portion of business school education is directly supported and funded by business organizations and individuals. This has led to research focusing on both operational and strategic issues directly relevant to the client base that seek consultancy services from business schools.

These two factors have ensured that for most traditional business schools, the understanding of politics in business is regarded as only a side issue at best and an aberration of the real issues at worst.[3] This is related to the rhetorical denial of the importance of politics in the business world itself. Politics is seen as a complication or unnecessary aspect of business life that reduces efficiency of business. On the other hand, a more positive development in IBS has been the development of business ethics at the core of many IBS programmes. This has provided an opportunity for politics to enter the framework of our understanding of IBS itself.

2.3.1 Differing approaches to the theory of international production

Arguably, the most influential scholars in understanding the causes and consequences of international production in the IBS field have been John Dunning and Michael Porter. In numerous works, Dunning has developed, elaborated and refined his 'eclectic' OLI paradigm. For the first time in IBS, Porter developed an explicit role for market structure on strategic management by developing the concept of competitive advantage. Thus while most MNE literature seeks to explain why firms decide to produce on a multinational basis Porter analysed the sources of relative success of some MNEs over others. We shall return to this distinction below. It is worth noting, however, that there have been other highly influential scholars in the field of IBS. In particular, we can draw attention to the research of Hymer (1968), Vernon (1971) and the many works by Mark Casson (Buckley and Casson 1976; Casson 1985, 1987, 1990).

Buckley (1992) claims that there is general agreement on an established theory of the MNE. It is based on a synthesis of the theory of location and competitive dynamics. In order to do this, however, we argue it is important to understand the different elements of this synthesis. Cantwell (1991) argues that we can consider theory on three levels: macroeconomic, which examines broad international trends, mesoeconomic, dealing with the relationship between a firm and the industry, and microeconomic, that emphasizes the growth of individual firms. Consequently, theories of trade (e.g. Ricardian, Hecksher-Ohlinian) and balance of payments (Mundell-Fleming, Portfolio Approach) dominate the macrolevel analysis. Mesolevel studies are grounded in industrial organization theories while micro-theories are based on microeconomics and organizational behavior. It would be fair to argue that IBS tends to underplay the macroeconomic explanations for international production, favouring the meso- and microlevel explanations.[4]

From this, we can develop three approaches to the theory of international production: market power motives, internalization approaches and competitive dynamic theories.

2.3.1.1 Market power motives

Hymer (1968) is largely associated with the development of our first approach. Market power understandings of international production are located in an understanding of the firm as a seeker of monopoly profits.[5] Thus, MNEs exist as a means of extending market power of firms. According to this approach, firms expand domestically in order to gain market share and market power through merger. This increases market concentration and hence the rate of profitability. Eventually, market size constraints in the domestic market force firms to invest their profits into foreign operations. This sets off a similar process of concentration in international markets. Where necessary, MNEs will leverage their dominant position in international markets in order to restrict competition domestically through international collusive agreements (Stocking and Watkins 1948).

It should be clear that the origins of this approach are related to both the insights of the classical political economists Adam Smith and Karl Marx and the industrial organization theory of structure-conduct-performance (SCP) as developed by Bain (1956). Importantly, Hymer's (1968) market-power understanding of the MNE provides an active role for strategy for the firm but unlike the SCP paradigm suggests that the causal link is from firm conduct to market structure. The Marxian interpretation of the Hymerian approach is that it explains a theory of dependency. Cox (1987) argued that MNEs create a transnational class of managers who extend domestic exploitation of labour to an international level. In this framework, corporate hierarchies are divided geographically into three subdivisions: corporate headquarters (executive managers), white-collar operational management in subsidiaries and blue-collar workers distributed globally. The result of this is that the core becomes increasingly developed and the periphery less developed (Eden and Potter 1993).

In a later work, Hymer (1968) developed a theory of the international division of labour. It combined his market-power concept with hierarchy and class conflict. He claimed that MNEs, in creating a world class of managers, generate conflict between this transnational managerial class and domestically based workers.[6] An extension of this theory suggests that we can explain the increasing flows of FDI to Asia and Latin America by the desire of MNE executive managers and local governing elites in these countries to exploit docile labour forces and low-cost raw materials (Yuan and Eden 1992).

2.3.1.2 Internalization motives

This market power approach would appear superficially clearly at odds with theories that explain the MNE in terms of raising internal efficiency. This latter group of theories relates to the benefits of internalizing transactions within the corporate space. The intellectual origins of these theories are in dissatisfaction with the neo-classical assumption that market transactions are costless.

Indeed, Ronald Coase's (1996) seminal work on the nature of the firm is unquestionably the starting point for this approach. Essentially, internalization approaches argue that where the costs of carrying out an administered, intra-firm transaction are lower than an arm's-length market transaction, firms will be motivated to internalize a market and raise the efficiency of the organization. Underpinning this approach is the work of Williamson (1975) who developed a theory of transaction costs. He argued that firms internalize market failures. The principal behavioural assumptions of this theory are that economic agents act rationally up to a point as they are faced with imperfect information, increasing complexity and limited capacity of organizations to cope with this (bounded rationality). Second, faced with imperfect information available in arm's-length markets, firms could be subject to opportunistic behavior of agents in the market (Williamson 1975). When extended to the MNE, Buckley and Casson (1976) argue that the firm is seeking to internalize an international market externality for strategic purposes. Thus, when an MNE is integrated vertically, the ownership of the raw material sources for its production reduces the market transaction costs in Williamson's framework. In order to operationalize this approach, we can draw a number of hypotheses. First, the greater the distance (both physical, cultural and organizational) between the MNE and its supplier, the greater is the incentive for the MNE to internalize its transactions. Second, the more frequent the transactions are, the more likely the MNE will seek to internalize the transaction. Third, the higher the technological complexity of the transaction, the higher is the desire for the MNE to internalize the transaction.

These hypotheses allow us to consider in which ways the MNE will seek the internalization of the transaction. It is important to realize that ownership is not the only means by which an MNE can internalize a transaction. Indeed, joint ventures and non-equity alliances can achieve a similar purpose. Jones et al. (1990) and Sako (1992) demonstrated in the car industry and microelectronics industry, respectively, that long-term contracting with suppliers, rather than ownership, has been a source of efficiency for Japanese MNEs.

At this stage, it is important to stress that while the market-power approach and the internalization approach appear to be at odds with each other they represent arguably two sides of the same coin. The obvious question to ask is when a vertically integrated MNE undertakes a further 'internalization' up- or downstream, is this to increase internal efficiency or to foreclose access to rivals? In other words, can internalization be for market-power reasons? A similar argument can be made for the horizontal acquisition of a foreign rival. One way of reconciling this issue is to recognize that the market-power approach is mainly concerned with the exclusion of potential rivals in the final product market whereas the transaction cost (internalization) approach emphasizes optimization in intermediate goods markets.[7] We shall return to this issue below.

A result of the debate over market power and internalization motives for the MNE was the development by Dunning (1981) of an 'eclectic paradigm'. Dunning (1988a: 117) claims that his work was not intended as a theory of MNE. Rather, it was a theory that explained the pattern and level of MNE activity. Nevertheless, while not becoming a universal theory of MNE, the eclectic paradigm became a useful tool for empirical investigation of the shortcomings and strengths of theories of international production.

The paradigm has been called the 'OLI' paradigm relating to the three sets of advantages that MNEs possess. These are ownership, location and internalization advantages. It is contended that MNEs have an advantage by 'owning' both unique intangible assets (e.g. technology) and joint ownership of complementary assets. These advantages are controlled by virtue of the internalization of these assets within a complex network. As with Williamson (1975), Dunning argues that transactional market failure is the main motive for the MNE. Location-based advantages are reasonably self-evident: the MNE chooses its location to maximize the benefits of the location for the internal efficiency of the firm. Eden and Potter (1993: 43) argue that MNE's location-based advantages are derived from three types of strategic investment. First, resource-seeking investments are where MNEs seek out the lowest cost source of inputs in the production process. This is frequently associated with extractive industries. Second, cost reducing investments relate to the search for low-cost inputs such as labour in order to produce semi-finished products for re-export. Lastly, we can consider market access investments. These exist to overcome trade barriers and to provide an initial foothold for the MNE in the foreign market. Moreover, they can be used to serve local markets (e.g. bottling plants). More recently, Birkinshaw and Hood (1998) differentiated between two kinds of strategies of MNEs – market serving and resource-seeking. Arguably, service sector industries such as banking would be suited to market-serving strategies while resource-seeking strategies would be used in manufacturing (Akbar and McBride 2002).

As the OLI paradigm does not have an explicit theory of competition built into it, it can explain an internalization approach whereby the MNE displaces imperfect markets or a market power argument that posits that the MNE, by colluding and merging, is a cause of market failure. Thus, ownership advantages can be construed as efficiency enhancing measures or anti-competitive barriers to entry.

2.3.1.3 *Competitive dynamics and competitive advantage*

While the market power motive for the MNE implicitly examines the role of reducing competition and is therefore based on some underlying 'theory of the industry' we also need to examine theories that consider the MNE in the competitive environment, both as drivers of competition and how the MNE performs relative to its rivals in a competitive market. The latter is the concept of competitive advantage generated by Porter (1980, 1990).

The market-power school argues that internationalization of production lowers competition in world markets; competitive international industry perspectives contend the opposite: that the MNE is involved in intense rivalry with other MNEs and this drives the process of technological change. In a similar fashion, Vernon (1966, 1971 and 1979) developed the product life-cycle theory that explained the shift from specialized, location-restricted production based on high technology towards the mass production of standardized products produced in several locations around the world and eventually by many MNEs producing differentiated varieties based on similar technologies. The technology of production in this model shifts from high human capital-intensive and R&D-intensive inputs towards high capital-intensity (the hallmark of mass production).

This idea was extended to consider how firms locate abroad as a risk-minimizing strategy. Graham (1978, 1985) argued that as the ratio of fixed to total costs rose, the possibility of 'cut-throat' price competition among oligopolistic rivals also rose.[8] Thus MNEs, as insurance against this outcome, would engage in intra-industry production.[9]

The role of technology is also an important element in the development of international production. There is a consensus in the literature that technological development is a cumulative process (Nelson and Winter 1977; Pavitt 1987). This implies that new technologies emerge out of a process of accumulated learning. Arguably, firms choose different production locations in order to benefit from localized centres of technological excellence.[10] Finally, it is possible to tie the concept of technological development with internalization motives. By creating a network of technological centres, the MNE is better able to control and leverage the benefits of R&D. This would be more costly if the firm had to acquire the technology in a market transaction.

Porter's works (1980, 1990) are arguably one of the most crucial contributions to the IBS literature. Porter developed the concept of the 'value chain'. This consists of a series of activities – either primary or support activities.[11] An MNE must choose the shape and length of its value chain with the overall objective of maximizing value-added from its activities. In his analytical framework, he placed a substantial emphasis on how market structure constrains the actions of MNEs. His 'Five Forces' model is regarded as a central analytical tool in IBS. He argued that firms are influenced by the degree of competition from buyers and sellers, the degree of product differentiation and the nature of entry and exit barriers in the industry. Consequently, the MNE can adopt four strategies: global cost leadership (selling a wide range of products globally); global segmentation (selling a narrow range of products worldwide or wide set of products in a narrow range of countries); protected markets (seeking shelter from competition through government-imposed barriers); and national responsiveness (developing products that meet local needs in particular countries) (Porter 1980: 46–9). An important implication of Porter's work is that some MNEs are more successful than others not because of problems of internal strategy and operational considerations but because of inappropriate strategies in the face of the market structure they face. This argument ran in the face of a considerable amount of prescriptive work on MNE strategy that focused on internal sources of strategic failure, e.g. Tilles (1963), Mintzberg (1973) and Prahalad and Hamel (1990).

2.3.2 Controversies in the theory of international production

There are arguably two controversies in the development of a theory of international production: the relationship between internalization and market structure and the relationship between internalization and competitive advantage.

As discussed in some detail above, we can draw a distinction between theories of the MNE based on those based on internalization and those based on market power. The political economy of this distinction is important. Depending on whether the incentives for MNE activity are derived from market power or internal efficiency motives, we should consider the implications of the MNE for economic and societal welfare. Arguably, the gains to internal efficiency derive from a replacement of an imperfect external market or the creation of a new allocation mechanism that did not exist previously. The losses caused by MNE activity could arguably be more widespread. First, MNE activity can be the result of a desire to extract monopolistic rents either through horizontal acquisition (final product market concentration) or through vertical integration (market foreclosure). Second, by internalizing a collusive agreement, MNEs make the enforcement of collusion more effective (Buckley 1992). Third, Marxian critics of the MNE argue that it exists to extend exploitation of workers across borders – a necessary feature of capitalism. In particular, Cowling and Sugden (1987) argue that the MNE exists to weaken the power of labour by diversifying production across countries. This allows owners to extract greater profits by driving down wages. The tendency of MNEs to concentrate markets through acquisition further intensifies this process (Galbraith 1971).

We need to consider the second 'controversy': between internalization and competitive advantage. Internalization theories of the MNE argue that the growth of the MNE relative to markets is determined by its internalization decisions: the firm grows by internalizing transactions and replacing imperfect markets. By contrast, Porter's approach suggests that the competitive advantage of a firm (its *sine qua non* cause of growth) is relative to other firms. In other words, it is related to firm-specific advantages that are not easily imitable. In fact, a deeper consideration of the difference reveals that competitive advantage in the Porter framework implies that market imperfections are the source of competitive advantage. Thus, the possession of superior technology is a source of competitive advantage. We can in fact therefore interpret internalization as a competitive weapon and therefore a pursuit of competitive advantage. Thus, it is often claimed that Japanese vertical *keiretsu* are a source of competitive advantage for Japanese companies relative to their US and European counterparts.

2.4 Developmental avenues in understanding the MNE

Buckley (1992: 6) suggests: 'political and social variables require more attention' in our understanding of the MNE. Indeed, as the IPE literature is beginning to suggest, MNEs are becoming central players in the world political economy. We shall argue in Chapter 3 that, in fact, the existing IBS literature ignores a potential benefit of MNE activity from the perspective of the introduction of higher standards of regulation. We will posit a theory that demonstrates that where MNEs are present in countries seeking to raise regulatory standards to higher foreign standards, MNEs can facilitate this process when they use higher standards as a tool of competitive rivalry. This provides an excellent source of synthesis between the IPE and IBS literatures. This is because it allows us to focus on largely technical aspects of corporate strategy while at the same time considering its impact on political processes. It is innovative in the sense that it is different from current research that emphasizes the direct political role of MNEs as 'lobbyists'.

Before we can do this, we need to consider current research on the political role of the MNE. The literature on this is broad and considerable. In a sense, this represents our consideration of the IPE literature dealing with the MNE. We will focus on the role of MNEs in affecting and influencing public policy. Consequently, we will not examine the critical developmental, the dependency and core–periphery literatures.[12]

2.5 The political role of the MNE

The current phase of globalization has created new transnational political spaces that have not been filled by states' regulatory capacity. Deregulation and increasing competition in the world political economy have meant that states have lost traditional control of markets thus creating new forms of market-based regulation on a multilateral and supranational level. Second, IOs have, to a degree, filled the policy vacuum left behind by retreating state regulations in a range of economic policy areas both on a regional and global level. Regionally, the growth and success of the European Union (EU) and the North American Free Trade Agreement (NAFTA) are examples of states ceding policy sovereignty.

On a global level, the increasing importance of policy prescriptions from the IMF and World Bank, with their emphasis on fiscal austerity and privatization, is another remarkable feature of the way in which states have allowed policy sovereignty to be shifted to supranational levels. In the case of the IMF and World Bank, Jan-Aart Scholte's (1996, 2000) research on the relationship between civil society and IOs demonstrates the increasing concern shown by IOs that they may not be accountable to civil society in the way democratic states have been historically.

An important implication of these two changes in the world political economy has been that traditional ways in which the relationships between public policy-makers (implicitly political in its aims at the level of states) and non-state actors (not necessarily explicitly political) need reconsideration.

Assigning an explicit (and implicit) role for non-state actors in the discipline of international relations has recently experienced significant attention in a range of sub-fields within the discipline. One of the most commonly observed claims in the discipline has been an apparent 'realist' or 'neo-realist' bias in the study of international politics. Sinclair (1999) observes that whenever it is clear that political agency is apparent in non-state entities, the discipline has tended to eschew undertaking systematic study of the phenomenon because it would require both methodologically and substantively difficult tasks. Many IPE scholars have preferred to remain within the 'safe' boundaries of analysing the role of the state with its well-defined institutional frameworks and well-established theories and explanations for behaviour. Even those scholars seeking to go beyond a realist strait-jacket by focusing on 'international regimes' (Keohane and Nye 1990; Ruggie 1989) have not paid explicit attention to non-state actors in a systematic way.

Having pointed out these apparent shortcomings, nevertheless, there has been important progress in the literature (Baron 1995, 1997; Dunning 1997; Maxwell et al. 1997; Globerman and Shapiro 1999; Hocking and McGuire 2001). Among scholars in the civil society literature, there has always been an explicit recognition and understanding that the state is far from a unitary actor in the international system. It has therefore been necessary to apply and modify sociological methods and theories that have traditionally been used to analyse 'domestic' societies to constellations of social behaviour at an international level (Scholte 1996, 2000; Shaw 1999). In terms of non-state actors, a significant focus has been on so-called NGOs such as international advocacy groups like Greenpeace or a more systemic and theoretical debate on what (if anything) constitutes 'global civil society'. Neo-Gramscian scholars such as Stephen Gill have paid attention to non-state power and agency in the international system but again the focus has been somewhat of a macro- or systemic-level approach rather than a sector-specific one. The explicit normative agenda of neo-Gramscians has been to critique the nature of global capitalism and the need for international society to reform the global capitalist economy.

Outside of the neo-Gramscian debate, Susan Strange was probably the greatest advocate of the need for systematic study of the political role of economic agents in the international system. In many published works (e.g. Strange 1986, 1996, 1998a, 1998b; Stopford and Strange 1991), she consistently observed that firms play a crucial role in the political structure of the world economy by directly influencing state policy-makers through well-established mechanisms of political influence. As importantly, however, Strange also emphasized that as the process of globalization has intensified, there has been a shift in political power relations between the state and non-state actors. Explicitly critiquing realist and neo-realist methodology, Strange argued that the state was no longer the predominant actor in the world political economy. Rather, the state is at best an equal partner; at worst a subordinate to new forms of political agency in the world political economy exercised by the MNE or supranational political institutions (e.g. the EU). In her path-breaking study with John Stopford (Stopford and Strange 1991), it was elegantly and effectively demonstrated that the GPE was witnessing a new form of 'triangular diplomacy' (state–state; state–firm; firm–firm) in which states 'competed' with each other to capture the benefits of the activities of MNEs. This competition emerges as a direct result of the ability of the MNE to exercise political power over states and by firms' ability to form alliances that cross territorially bounded notions of political authority. Another significant contribution of this work was that it made use of country- and sector-specific and empirically rich material to illustrate these conceptual claims.

Stopford and Strange's (1991) central finding that states have experienced a loss in their ability to control resources in the world political economy echoes in the work of Palan and Abbot (1998). As the title of the study suggests, Palan and Abbot argue that states no longer set the terms of activity of firms within their boundaries. On the contrary, the study suggests that states actually set up regulatory and legal frameworks that favour the business objectives of firms in order to attract these MNEs to produce within the territorial boundaries governed by the state. In the regulatory literature, the result of inter-state competition is referred to as 'regulatory competition'. The implicit (and normative) argument against regulatory competition is that it leads to lowering standards for environmental, labour market and social standards as firms' profit functions do not incorporate the inclusion of these costs in the strategy of the firms concerned. They will thus choose locations where the lowest regulatory standards are present.

Cutler et al. (1999) provide a detailed sector-specific study of the role of the firm in international politics. It offers both theoretical and empirical material on this issue. Its central aim is to explore the phenomenon of international private authority and asks whether this form of private authority can and should provide the necessary collective goods for the GPE. They argue that private authority is granted authority because of technical expertise and historical practices that legitimate this behaviour and explicit or implicit power granted by states (Cutler et al. 1999: 335).

2.6 The contribution of European Studies

There is a vigorous debate in the social sciences as to whether European Studies is a discipline or a sub-field of international relations.[13] Nevertheless, the nature of the European integration process, which this book examines empirically, has meant that the role of the MNE has been especially prevalent.

Keohane (1984) and more recently Moravscik (1998) have argued that European integration has resulted largely out of economic interdependence and that this interdependence has required states to 'pool' sovereignty in order maintain a weakened form of sovereignty. Moreover, states co-operate as it is in their self-interest to do so, thus maintaining methodologically one of the central tenets of neo-realism. According to Moravscik (1998), even cases cited by critics of neo-realism as proof of the supranationality undermining the state against its will are exceptions and largely because of economic interdependence specific to the period.

Despite these arguments, one of the most intellectually valuable consequences of the study of EU integration has been the extension of political methodology used to explain how states are influenced by domestic non-state actors at a 'European level'. As states have co-operated to regulate economic activity at a European level, MNEs have formed associations and advocacy organizations in order to influence the formulation of that regulation both in an informal and formal manner. In recent years, both Wallace and Young (1997) and Middlemas (1995) have demonstrated both formal and informal attempts by business associations to influence policy-making in the European Union. Coen (1997) has also explicitly studied what he terms the 'European business lobby' as a separate entity from national lobby groups.

Indeed, it should be expected that European MNEs would have both different substantive and normative agendas from their national counterparts. On a sector-by-sector basis, it should be expected that differing national agendas related to relative competitiveness, differences in the use of production technologies, degree of 'openness' of the national industry and other historical legacies play a role in the agendas set by national associations and firms. Milner (1988) studied trade preferences of firms and demonstrated that traditional theories that suggested that domestic producers, when faced with trade liberalization, would resist such deregulation fearing loss of market share to foreign rivals was not as certain as previously claimed. She showed the picture to be considerably more complicated in that MNEs would pursue a more diversified policy agenda if their business strategies required a multinational production and distribution presence. In this situation, the MNE would prefer a liberal trade policy across the board as it allowed them to maximize the benefits of the multinational nature of its strategy. By contrast, a firm that was strongly nationally based whose major customers were domestic and who did not rely heavily upon imports of sub-components would most likely favour a protectionist policy.

Thus on a supranational level, MNEs are not necessarily likely to conform to traditional concepts of industry as inherent 'opponents of free trade'. Rather, a range of preferences from liberal to protectionist should be observed.

In the context of the EU, this transnational diversity is complemented by policy-making that is technocratic. This is probably a result of the nature of integration that has hitherto been largely economic. Arguably, the success of policy formulation has been its emphasis on 'low politics' such as the mutual recognition of technical standards rather than the pursuit of 'high' political aims that have been the traditional domain of states, e.g. foreign policy. Given the technocratic nature of the policy-making, the role of industry 'expertise' in the formulation of appropriate regulation at the EU level has been central. During the process leading up to the signing of the Single European Act,[14] the role of technocratic expert agencies and forums was crucial in the creation of EU-wide 'minimum standards'. Such forums included CENELEC that was set up to develop EU standards on electricity rules, and ESPRIT, that aimed to encourage research and development in high technology. These groups comprised national representatives of member states but also senior representatives of those involved specifically in those industries covered by the group.

Thus the MNEs in the sectors subject to EU regulation were directly involved in the development of standards for these industries. The official, and partly justified, reason for the need for industry experts was that many of the rules and standards being 'harmonized' were too complicated for non-experts to generate and govern. It was experts more closely acquainted with technological understanding of the industry who could best offer guidance on the 'best practice' standard for the EU. Many of the experts themselves had worked for large European MNEs.

Where MNEs influence governments is in their ability to foster economic growth and increase the 'international' strength of a particular country. In this framework, there appear to be few avenues in which the role of MNE could either transcend national demands and preferences or pursue agendas that may be contrary to domestic or state preferences.

Arguably, political lobbying by MNEs ensures that where governmental regulation impacts on the business that they undertake, the regulatory framework is set up to maximize the benefits to the MNE concerned. As Moran (1998) has shown, this can be regarded as a form of political risk management where firms aim either to pre-empt future regulation with policy lobbying aimed at influencing the final future legislation adopted or by continually applying pressure to modify existing legislation.

The persuasive strength that MNE possesses is that it has sectoral and technical expertise that is indispensable to policy-makers. As regulation becomes ever more complex, sector-specific expertise becomes more valuable to the MNE in its attempts to influence the framing of policy. Examples of this abound. For example, in the telecommunications sector, there is a brisk debate over appropriate regulation for certain services such as mobile telephony. MNEs play a crucial role in arguing that their understanding of the industry technology will help policy-makers frame a 'best practice' regulation. A recent case of this was a UNICE[15] paper entitled 'UNICE calls for an alternative to regulation'. UNICE argues that regulation is an outdated concept in many areas of industry and commerce and that 'co-regulation and self-regulation' are a more appropriate framework for market transactions.[16]

This 'pro-market' and technocratic orientation of policy-making is also testament to the structural political power of MNEs. This is partly due to changes in the governance of the world political economy that have granted increased power to MNEs in addition to the specific aspects of the EU integration process.[17]

It is important to link MNE pressure for the adoption of technical standards with the competitive advantage or disadvantage that they possess relative to their competitors. Thus, MNEs will seek to have regulation designed to maximize returns to their own production process or service system. In a case where the firms possess a competitive advantage in their production system, they will seek to have this standard 'locked in' to regulations designed to cover the industry concerned. A similar argument can be forwarded where MNEs have a competitive disadvantage. Thus, MNEs using uncompetitive technology may attempt to influence policy-makers to adopt their standard even if it is inferior to other existing or potentially new standards.[18]

Theoretically, one of the objectively positive outcomes of CLO pressure to adopt 'best practice' that is *genuinely* best practice, is that it drives regulatory standards upwards in the sense that policy-makers will be able to offer the most efficient standard (to which we shall turn in Chapter 3). This is particularly relevant where states are adopting new supranational legislation by entering it into national legislation. In other academic disciplines such as economics and IBS, academicians support this 'pro-market' view arguing that leaving regulation, in the extreme self-regulation, to market participants is likely to produce 'optimal' results.[19] An example of this would be the Basle Concordat agreed in 1986 by the Basle Committee, which comprises central bankers from member countries of the Bank for International Settlements (BIS). This supranational concordat, while not being officially internationally enforceable law, was adopted by all the members of the BIS as best practice standards for capital adequacy supervision of the commercial banking sector.[20] Alternatively, if MNE pressure 'locks in' a standard that favours an inefficient outcome, then the effects on technical progress and consumer interests could be negative.

Sandholz and Zysman (1989: 128) argued that industrial elites had supported the EU Commission efforts to pursue integration. Haas (1964: 353) claims that industrial elites accepted the emergence of a supranational authority 'from whom favors must be asked and advantages extracted or whose policies must be opposed'.

Cawson (1995, 1997) makes an explicit attempt to analyse how large company corporate structure develops political lobbying strategies. He argued that individual MNE power granted it asymmetric access to EU institutions. By focusing on high-technology sectors, Cawson attempted to demonstrate that large firms in addition to trade associations actively lobby governments.[21] Instead, he shows that Phillips, a large European electronics MNE, as a single entity gained privileged access to the EU Commission. In fact, as Cawson illustrates, Phillips regarded its representation to Brussels as its 'Embassy to the EU' (Cawson 1995: 198). Not only did Phillips provide technical assistance to the EU Commission in helping specific staff formulate policy but it provided *stagiaire* training for Commission employees.

Cowles (1997) traces the development of organized industrial interests in the EU from its creation in the 1950s to the present day. She argues that the European Roundtable of Industrialists (ERT) was probably one of the most influential groups to have emerged. The ERT consisted of senior business leaders from EU MNEs. Their influence derived from the transnational and technocratic nature of their agenda – that of focusing the minds of EU policy-makers on the need to complete the Common Market. The ERT embarked on an unprecedented campaign in the early 1980s to demonstrate the need for a new 'technological' Europe (Cowles 1997: 129). The message sent by the ERT was simple, to quote Cowles: 'support the single market programme or European industry will invest elsewhere' (Cowles 1997: 130).[22]

Coen and Grant (2000) examine the Transatlantic Business Dialogue (TABD) and its relationship with the EU Commission. The TABD was an institution bringing together CEOs of major North American and European MNEs who had significant commercial interest in transatlantic commerce. Noted by Al Gore as an influential gathering, the TABD was described by him as 'a good place for the rest of industry to bring pressure to bear' (Coen and Grant 2000: 4) in the context of the generation of third-generation technology for mobile telephony. Overall then, the existing literature has highlighted an important role for MNEs in regulatory decision-making generally and EU policy-making specifically.

2.7 States' preferences and policies towards MNEs

Sections 2.4 and 2.5 have examined the literature on how and why MNEs influence states and public policy-making. It is also important for a synthesis of the IBS and IPE literature to consider what governmental authority seeks to do in its relationship with MNEs. Without this discussion, we could mislead the reader into thinking that we consider the MNE–governmental relationship is one-way.

Vernon (1971) is regarded as one of the first seminal discussions on the role of states and how they influence MNEs. As claimed in a recent article (Vernon 1993: 19): '[his] conviction [...] was that manifest technical advantages of large enterprises and of strong governments will lead men in the future to insist on both'. Explicitly, Vernon is arguing that far from governments disappearing from the picture, they need to exist in order for society to benefit directly from MNEs.

Gilpin (1975) argued that strong states (explicitly in his study, the USA) could use their national MNEs to spread their influence around the world as a means of extending their state power. Safarian (1993) claims that public authority has an ongoing love–hate relationship with the MNE. Furthermore he argues that governments seek more than just economic benefits from MNEs, and therefore a conventional neo-classical economic analysis will miss a substantial degree of the intentions of public policy. He posits that in addition to the economic benefits of investment that MNEs bring, states either encourage or discourage MNE activity as a function of the role of an attempt to balance competing interests among various social actors. This can encompass electoral, ideological, bureaucratic and material pressures.

Some interest groups are critical of MNEs because of the loss of sovereignty that the presence of MNEs implies. Governments are concerned especially by the perception that their capacity to make public policy is constrained by MNEs. As we shall argue in Chapter 3, MNEs facilitate public policy-making under certain conditions.

Furthermore, social changes brought about by MNEs may face resistance from national or regional cultures that fear losing relevance in their society. It can indeed be a source of international trade conflict in sectors closely related to culture such as audiovisual services (Akbar 2001).

Doremus et al. (1998) argue that far from the state losing control of its public policy-making capacity, the fact that MNEs remain largely embedded in strong national cultures means that there remains considerable scope for the state to influence the activities of MNEs:

> At a time when critics are seeking points of resistance to pressures associated with the word globalization, we find systematic national differentiation in the very corporations that many believe to be the progenitors of a new global economic infrastructure. (Doremus et al. 1998: 12)

They further contend that a combination of corporate inertia, path dependence and the legacy of past choices ensures that the MNE remains closely tied to its home state. Based on an analysis of US, Japanese and German MNEs, they found that these firms remained closely linked to cultural and ideological underpinnings of the society from which they emerged. This was reflected in differing governance, financing and ownership structures of these three 'national' MNEs.

Where states, by themselves, are unable to regulate the activities of MNEs as effectively as in the past, it is increasingly the case that they are turning to bilateral, minilateral and multilateral forms of co-operation.[23] While critics of these agreements argue that they reflect the vested interests of MNEs, the fact that states decide to co-operate or when to agree to new supranational institutions for the governance of economic activity suggests a pervasive role for regulation of market outcomes.[24] It certainly undermines the 'straw man' perception of the world political economy becoming radically different because of globalization as depicted by Barnet and Cavanagh (1994), Greider (1992) and most famously by Fukuyama (1992).[25]

At the same time, we do not suggest that nothing has changed. The process of international economic deregulation, as patchy and piecemeal as it has been, has for significant parts of the world political economy created far-reaching changes in the ways of MNEs as political actors influence policy-making. As we have attempted to show above, the literature on this issue is significant, evolving and arguably growing in importance as IPE theory develops.

Once again, however, we are not suggesting, as Strange (1996) does, that the world political economy is undergoing secular irreversible change towards a more economically liberal form where MNEs will be as powerful political actors as states. The future evolution of the world political economy is unlikely to be mapped purely by reference to past and current trends. However, what we are seeing is a current phase in which public policy-making is increasingly technocratic and therefore creates unrivalled political influence for the MNE. Moreover, state actions are evolving to take into account this and other trends. Thus, the resort to limited regional and multilateral integration is a means of preserving authority albeit in a modified form. This is an issue that we shall refer to in considerable detail in the concluding chapter of this book.

2.8 An interdisciplinary synthesis of IPE and IBS understanding of the MNE

Eden and Potter (1993: 33–4) claim that IBS approaches to understanding the MNE constitute predominantly liberal perspectives from IPE. This, they argue, is because of the ideological bias of IBS as a discipline devoted to 'problem solving' from the perspective of international managers. This is a somewhat reductionist view of the increasingly broad church of IBS. Precisely as the MNE has extended its reach in the world political economy both geographically and in terms of its effect on policy, substantial pressure has been placed on the MNE to become a 'corporate citizen' and to broaden its concept of ownership from narrow shareholder interests towards broader stakeholder interests.[26] This normative shift has allowed for a broader interpretation of the concept of IBS and the objectives of teaching and research in the field.[27] Business ethics as a sub-field of IBS has become incorporated in many leading MBA programmes around the world and there are notable institutions devoted to the study of responsible international business.[28]

Moving away from normative aspects of IBS, the increasing number of IPE specialists and political scientists now based at international business schools suggests that as IBS seeks out new research agendas, it is almost inevitable that political and societal aspects of IBS will become important. As Buckley (1992) suggests, this can only occur if there is an explicit attempt at developing an interdisciplinary framework. As Buckley (1992: 15) states, this process is fraught with many problems:

> Researchers in international business will be familiar with the key difficulty in this area – the argument that the 'cobbler should stick to his last' and warnings not to dabble in other experts' areas. It can be met by the individual scholar going back to the drawing board and learning anew. Or it can be met by the building of interdisciplinary teams and confronting the language, culture and other boundaries which separate disciplines.

Strange (1996), Cutler et al. (1999) and Akbar (2001) among others have identified that critique and prescription within IPE have constrained the analysis of the MNE. Hocking and McGuire (2001) refer to the need for 'postmodern' trade policy analysis that moves beyond traditional state orientation. There has been a tendency for IPE to rely upon safe boundaries within which to study. At the same time, a form of intellectual snobbery about the 'quality' of IBS research has clouded many IPE scholars' attitudes towards interdisciplinary co-operation. However, it would be foolhardy to ignore the intellectual and scholarly value-added of collaboration between IBS and IPE as disciplines. This is for several reasons.

First and foremost, the disciplines are essentially interested in the same actors. They may take different normative perspectives on the intentions, policies and outcomes of the actors concerned but they both recognize, more or less, their existence and importance.

Second, both IPE and IBS are 'non-traditional' disciplines when compared to political science, sociology, economics, law and anthropology. They therefore have less intellectual baggage and dogma than these more classical of the social science disciplines.

Third, IPE and IBS are interdisciplinary concepts. They can recognize the validity of moving beyond rigid disciplinary straitjackets in order to enhance our understanding of theory and practice.

Fourth, from an empirical standpoint, business schools and IPE departments have the potential for considerable complementarity. *De minimis*, the contacts with industry that business schools offer are a useful source of primary material for an IPE scholar.

This book aims at contributing to this synthesis by developing a theoretical approach to understanding how MNEs influence the technical and procedural convergence and implementation of new regulatory standards. It explicitly attempts to consider how MNE strategy, a field of study traditionally belonging to IBS, impacts on legislative and regulatory change, itself traditionally the preserve of IPE and political science. As will be examined in some detail in Chapter 4, its empirical setting is the current process of EU enlargement to incorporate states from CEE. As we explain in Chapter 3 below, this empirical case is both an excellent test of our theoretical claims and also allows us to enrich the emerging synthesis of IPE and IBS as disciplines.

2.9 Conclusion

This chapter has outlined in detail past and current approaches taken by IBS and IPE in explaining the existence, actions and outcomes of the MNE. We argue that a synthesis of the two disciplines is necessary to understand the political role of MNEs. There is an emerging and encouragingly analytical literature based on this synthesis. Its origins are to be found in the work of Vernon (1971), Hymer (1968) and Strange (1988a). This has been extended in recent years by numerous scholars referred to above. Both IBS and IPE scholars, thankfully, recognize the need to extend their analytical scope further. This is a testament to the development of the two interdisciplinary subjects themselves.

In Chapter 3, we will offer our theoretical framework, which, we believe, is based on an explicit synthesis of the two disciplines. While considerable work has been done on our understanding of the MNE as a direct political actor, we have chosen to focus on the 'indirect' influence that MNEs possess through their strategies for competitive advantage. This exercise is what we turn to next.

3
Regulatory Convergence: Processes and Dynamics

3.1 Introduction

As we discussed in the previous chapter, there is an emerging consensus in the study of the world political economy that firms should be considered as transnational political actors. This is a response to empirical evidence that continues to undermine an exclusive state-centric approach to international relations. Consequently, considerable conceptual and theoretical work has been undertaken to understand the mechanisms by which the firm, as a commercial, non-governmental entity, can impact on political processes. This has been underpinned by considerable empirical research, predominantly on a case-study basis, which highlights and validates these theoretical claims. In this chapter, we aim to build on the theoretical and conceptual debate on the firm as a transnational political actor.[1] Relatively little research has been done on the indirect influence of firms through their role in standard setting and regulation as part of their strategy for competitive advantage.

Murphy (1995) is a detailed analysis of the ways in which firms use standards as a means of competitive advantage. The study terms this 'regulatory competitive advantage'. This chapter contributes to the literature on the indirect, technocratic influence of the firm in transnational politics by building on this concept. Conventional wisdom on the relationship between firms and regulation is that firms exploit lower regulatory standards across states in order to lower their production costs. The net result of this is that states compete with each other to offer lower standards of regulation in order to attract foreign direct investment (FDI). This phenomenon, often referred to as regulatory competition, is viewed differently by scholars. Neo-liberal economists and public choice theorists argue that regulatory competition is a good thing as it forces the most 'efficient' standard on to markets because of the underlying assumption that markets allocate resources more efficiently than the state.[2] Political scientists who focus on the impact of 'market failure' on ecology, for example, argue that regulatory competition, by encouraging states to undersupply regulation, actually encourages environmental damage by lowering standards of regulation. In this scenario, firms are seen as undermining the protection of environmental, worker and human rights.

While it is clear that there is significant empirical evidence to suggest that indeed some multinational enterprises (MNEs) have exploited regulatory differences between markets, this chapter aims to offer a different theoretical perspective. We will suggest that, in fact, MNEs under a set of given conditions actually use higher regulatory standards as tools of competitive rivalry. Where the presence of MNEs in domestic industries is significant, the result of this is that states find the introduction of higher standards of regulation less costly in terms of the costs imposed on the domestic industry. This is because many of the firms of the sector may already be producing at this standard as part of their existing business survival strategy. Thus, rather than undermining domestic standards of regulation, investment liberalization actually raises standards. The implications for our understanding of international political economy (IPE) are potentially far-reaching. First, as a discipline, IPE needs to look more closely at the political economy of corporate strategy in terms of its role in influencing international regulatory norms. Second, there is a substantial area for fruitful research in the role of economic 'conflict resolution' where the presence of MNEs leads to 'harmonization' of regulatory standards between countries, thus reducing what Ostry (1994) terms 'System Friction'. Third, where regulatory convergence is enhanced by the transborder activity of MNEs, the politics of standard setting is impacted by the business activities of the foreign firms. In particular, political pressure for protection from trade and investment liberalization will be reduced as the source of political pressure – industry and economic adjustment costs – will be lower. This is a corollary of Milner (1988) and Milner and Yoffie (1989) who posed the claim that if domestically incorporated firms relied heavily on export markets for their profitability, they would paradoxically resist calls for trade protection. A similar case would be for firms dependent on imports of semi-finished products.

The chapter is organized as follows. Part one provides an overview of the related literature in this area. Part two provides a detailed discussion of key terms and concepts used in this chapter as well as the theoretical approach offered in this chapter. Part three contains concluding remarks and directions for future research.

3.2 The current state of the art

An understanding of the relationship between business strategy and regulatory convergence requires an understanding and an appreciation of a broad literature as set out in Chapter 2. Not only do scholars have to understand and be able to conceptualize the strategy process (Porter 1980), they also have to be able understand the institutional and political dynamics of regulation. They also have to have a grasp of conceptualizations of the dynamics of the GPE more generally (e.g. Palan and Abbot 1998; Strange 1986, 1996, 1998a, 1998b). Furthermore, it is vital to emphasize the political nature of business strategy not in terms of conventional concepts of politics but in terms of the technocratic role that firms play in setting the industry standard (e.g. Akbar 2001). To the extent that once the standard is set, there will be a net outcome of industry gainers and losers, the political impact will be as a consequence of political pressure on states to deal with the losers. Thus where an industry in an economy is dominated by industry leaders (in the transnational market sense), then their political influence comes from their ability to set a 'global' or 'regional' standard by forcing other firms, if they wish to compete, to adopt the standard. This imposes an adjustment process on rival firms and may lead to political pressure for protection.

Arguably, given the trade and investment liberalization since the 1980s, the ability of domestic firms of the non-MNE variety to seek protection in the traditional sense has declined. This implies that the ability of the MNE to be a standard setter in the world economy has increased considerably. Indeed, since the 1980s, the role of international standard setting bodies in a range of sectors from banking to telecommunications at a global and regional (e.g. European) level has increased substantially. This is in part a cause of and a response to the increasing interpenetration of markets by MNEs. Thus states that traditionally may have been able to shelter domestic firms through domestic standard setting are either willingly or unwillingly allowing a transnational standard setting process to set the terms of domestic competition.

This enhances the role of the MNE in the regulatory convergence process in that the presence of MNEs in domestic economies facilitates the process of convergence of standards by bringing with them the 'best practice' in the industry to the local market.

As is well known, the theory of international production has undergone considerable development since the work of Hymer (1968) and Vernon (1971). Arguably, Buckley and Casson (1976) provide the seminal study of the causes and implications of MNE production. Michael Porter's works on business strategy is also regarded in the international business literature as the path-breaking and systematic work in the area (1980 and 1990). Whereas Buckley and Casson (1976) emphasized internal efficiency arguments for the internalization of transactions and hence the creation of the MNE, Porter attempted to evaluate how market structure constrains the strategy of MNEs. In Porter (1980), he outlined the most rigorous framework to date in international business for explaining how competition emerges, how firm strategy is endogenous to the process of competition and within the prescriptive realm, and what steps need to be taken for successful strategy. John Dunning (1981, 1997, 1988a, 1988b), for his part, developed an eclectic paradigm that sought to provide an overarching framework in which both Hymerian market power arguments and internalization motives could be reconciled (Cantwell 1991).

Significant work followed Porter's first study (Caves 1982; Doz 1986; Prahalad and Doz 1987). Porter himself followed up his first work with a more prescriptive study in 1986 dealing with concrete steps to be taken by firms to achieve competitive advantage. He then wrote a related work in 1990 on how states can create competitive advantage in terms of attracting companies to invest and produce in their domestic economies.

Stopford and Strange (1991) is a seminal work on the bargaining relationship between states and firms. Getz (1997) analyses political action in corporate strategy while related research on the relationship between corporate strategy and trade policy is presented in Rugman and Verbeke (1990, 1998). The specific case of intellectual property rights is dealt with by Sell (1999). There has been a flood of research on the role of MNEs and their relationships with host governments, e.g. Sanyal and Guvenli (2000), Globerman and Shapiro (1999). All of this valuable research focuses on the direct impact of the firm on international politics. This chapter seeks to go beyond this to focus on the indirect impact of corporate strategy on the political processes and effects of regulatory convergence. The literature on core competence and strategy can also shed light on this issue. Prahalad and Hamel (1990) argue that a successful strategy of a firm is based on the development and exploitation of core competence. A core competence is defined as a process or ability that a firm possesses that grants it a competitive advantage over rivals.[3] The link to standards can be made by considering how a production or service standard can create a competitive advantage if this standard is based on the core competence of a firm or a group of firms in an industry. An example of this is the provision of after-sales parts and repairs in the automotive sector. Parts and repairs are a core competence of an automotive value-chain. Automotive firms invest significant resources into developing parts and repairs for new automobiles. In order to appropriate as much of the value-added as possible in this process automotive assemblers have acquired legal right to exclusively supply registered repairers and thus to prevent copying and poor service provision.[4] In services that require a significant amount of 'over-the-counter' service, the role of service standards can allow firms to leverage their core competence.[5]

3.3 Definitions and theoretical propositions

Having outlined the current research that has been used to build the approach in our study, this section will develop more explicitly the theoretical approach taken. In order to do this, it is first necessary to define and develop some key terminology. First, we need to consider regulatory convergence. Regulation is taken as a broad definition. That is, regulation refers to rules governing the activities of firms in a given sector. This can relate to standards for production at a product and process level as well as rules on service provision in a given sector. This is a broader definition than that of regulation of natural monopolies. Often the term 'regulation' is useful in a transnational context in that transnational rules are developed to 'harmonize' or 'converge' differing national regulations.[6]

Convergence in this sense may imply two processes. First, it is possible to observe the partial or wholesale adoption of existing transnational rules as the basis for domestic industries. This has been the case where there are no existing national rules in place and where it has been 'easier' to adopt rules and regulations from either a transnational regime or other state-level rules. It can also feature in a process in which states are seeking to join multilateral regimes and organizations. Second, a process occurs through which standards become accepted as benchmarks because of their perception as 'best practice'. This can be related to technology, legal and ethical constraints or even history. Indeed, history matters because of the advantages that sometimes accrue to standards as 'first movers'. By being first into a given sector through a new standard, this sometimes emerges as the *modus operandi* for an industry by sheer numbers of companies and individuals making use of this standard.[7] Technology, and the leading and most efficient technology, will clearly play a determining role in the development of standards. This is because the given standard generates a competitive advantage to the firms developing and exploiting this standard. In order for other firms to compete, they may have to adopt similar technologies.[8]

Legal and ethical constraints are also important in the process of regulatory convergence. This is because society begins to develop guidelines on what is legal and ethical for firms to undertake. Where it is regarded that certain states or international organizations have rules that are ethically 'higher', political pressure from civil society may encourage other states to adopt those rules. There can also be commercial pressures brought to bear on states through the risk of trade and investment embargo for failure to implement higher ethical standards as well.

Thus given the definition and conceptual dynamics that underpin the process of regulatory convergence, it is now necessary to evaluate the role that firms play in that process and the political implications of this role.

In developing a strategy, there are set objectives and often a greater number of variables that go into the meeting of those given objectives. Our assumption is that firms develop or adopt standards as a vehicle for profit maximization. Whether profit maximization is the key variable for a firm is not a contentious issue in this context. It serves as a reliable proxy for some kind of optimization objective. Moreover, whether or not a firm optimizes is not strictly relevant in this instance. The assumption remains that firms use standard setting as a tool of competitive rivalry (and therefore optimization).

There is a conventional wisdom in neo-classical economics that firms seek profit maximization through cost minimization. This implies that when faced with a choice of adopting more costly 'higher' standards or lowering production costs by using a lower-standard, lower-priced product, firms will opt for the latter option. Thus, for example, firms will seek to minimize costs associated with production process standards by under-investing in environmentally sound technologies. This would certainly be the case where there is no domestic or internationally agreed regime on the standard. This is the phenomenon sometimes referred to as 'regulatory competition' or 'race towards the bottom'. However, where there are internationally agreed standards or where the destination of the products or services requires that firms produce to higher minimum standards, then firms can legitimately compete on 'quality' or production to the higher standard. A second situation in which it is likely that firms will use higher standards to compete is in service sectors where the essence of a quality service necessarily implies higher standards.

Thus, where existing regulations compel firms to meet those standards or service provision implies competition based on quality of service standard (as well as price), then it is likely that higher standards will necessarily emerge.

3.4 The model of the MNE and regulatory convergence

How does this link with the political and legislative process of regulatory convergence? For the purposes of illustration, we will assume that we examine the case of FDI and the part played by the MNE based locally. In order to highlight the first case of why higher standards emerge, we shall further assume that the MNE is seeking to compete in a service sector on the basis of higher service standards. When the MNE enters the market, its local rivals will need to respond to the new entrant. Assuming that the strategic variable is the service standard, there are two possible responses that local firms could choose. First, the default option is to recognize that the principal market for the foreign firm is a high-price niche service. The MNE does not therefore represent a threat to the local rivals. This means that there will be no market-led pressure for regulatory convergence. The local standards will remain unless there is a decision by legislators to adopt higher standards.

Second, the local firm, recognizing that the foreign firm could use higher standards to compete with local firms for domestic market share, will attempt to meet or surpass the foreign firm's standard. Here, standards will be driven up by the activities of both local and foreign firms. Crucially, this process will be initiated by the presence of foreign firms.

In a situation where there is political will to adopt higher international standards by a legislature, the fact that a foreign firm is already producing to that higher standard in the local market will facilitate the process of convergence to the higher international standard. This is because either local rivals will have adopted the higher standard as a means of survival or the foreign firm will dominate the local market by virtue of its higher standards. This will be further enhanced if it is clear to the local firms that at some stage in the future, the political will to introduce higher standards will lead to the necessary adoption of higher standards. This implies that local firms will need to prepare in advance.[9]

The important result of this process is that the adjustment costs associated by the regulatory convergence may be lower because of the presence of foreign firms who will attract resources in the sector away from local firms. Short-term unemployment resulting from competitive losses by the local firms will be mitigated by the hiring of workers by the foreign entrant. This will reduce political pressure for protection.[10] Thus rather than increasing political tensions domestically, the arrival of foreign companies will facilitate the legislative process towards higher standards, meeting less opposition from domestic industry in response to the regulatory convergence process.

Of course, if the assumptions proposed above are altered, we should see different outcomes. For example, if the industry has no existing transnational regime governing the standards used in the industry, then the possibility of MNEs exploiting lower standards may emerge.[11] This, in turn, may lead to political pressure domestically for the MNEs to be monitored more closely and could encourage political action internationally to draw attention to the activities of the MNE.[12]

If the MNE entry into the market is for predominantly local provision for local consumers, then the MNE may well adopt local standards. Generally, this becomes more important the larger the local market and, in the case of production rather than service provision, the smaller the export market for the MNE.[13] To further reinforce our analysis, it is now necessary to focus more specifically on the types of standards at hand. Again, some definitional exposition will aid the theoretical approach. By standards, we refer to the rules governing supply of a given product or service. How these standards emerge is a complex process beyond the scope of this chapter (and of our study in general) but some discussion of the kinds of standards we are examining is necessary. In this chapter, we are analysing principally three types of standards: process standards, product standards and service standards. It is possible that each of these types of standards could have different impacts on firm strategy. It is now necessary to take each of these in turn.

Process standards relate to the methods of production used by the firm. Thus, the aim of regulation in this sense is to influence the nature of inputs and how they are transformed into outputs. Regulators may be concerned with a range of issues here such as environmental impact of processes or health and safety in the production process. This can be especially relevant in the energy sector where the method of electricity generation can have a negative impact on the environment.

Product standards relate to the output of a firm's activities. The generation and regulation of product standards are more controversial than process standards. This is predominantly because of the ways in which product standards have been used as a form of non-tariff barrier to trade. They act in such a way as to require importers or MNEs who produce locally to meet the standards to be allowed to sell. In this instance, the standard is designed to require competitor foreign firms to change their products thereby raising their production costs so as to make it unprofitable to produce. Alternatively, product standards can be used as a genuine attempt to improve the quality standards of products in the interest of society. These can cover a range of areas including phytosanitary, recyclability, safety of usage relating to electrical products and environmental impact of usage. Where states agree to international accords on product standards such as ISO standards, it is less arguable that the standards are used as a non-tariff barrier as these standards are recognized across states. A similar case is that of mutual recognition. This is where states agree to set minimum standards but states are free to set higher standards as long as they recognize each other's and do not use their higher standard to prevent the sale of imported products.[14]

Given the growth of the service sector in the world economy accompanied by liberalization in the provision of services internationally, the role of service standards and competition in service sectors has increased in importance. Examples of service standards relate to financial services and the regulation of lending activities or telecommunication standards such as quality of Internet connection. For the purposes of this chapter, we argue that service standards are a direct feature of the activities of firms in their competitive rivalry. Thus, we argue that standards are driven upwards by competitive forces and consequently, where firms are unable to compete on service quality, they are either required to lower price if at all possible or exit the industry.

Taking each of these in turn, we shall now examine the role of how MNEs may actually facilitate the introduction of higher standards and the impact on a domestic industry. Once we have covered the scenarios, we add a further assumption that the target country for the MNE is seeking to sign international, multilateral or regional agreements on the harmonization of standards. With this assumption, we can offer more determinate outcomes.

In the case of process standards, it is likely that an MNE will use higher process standards in order to comply with rules related to both the local requirements and the rules on how products are produced in export markets. In other words, if the MNE is producing in order to export to other markets, we assume that the export markets have rules on the process used to produce the good.[15] There are numerous explanations for an MNE entry into a local market.[16] In the case below, implicitly we assume that the primary motivation for MNE entry is to benefit from lower factor costs such as access to lower cost labour.

In this scenario, the arrival of the MNE would lead to a raising of the process standard in the industry. The extent to which the standard would increase is a function of the reaction of the local firms. If they perceive the export markets of the MNE as being potential markets for themselves, they would follow suit and raise the process standard.

If they fear that the MNE would attempt to capture local market share by using the higher process standard, they would either be forced to lower price that could lead to losses and eventually exit or be forced to raise the process standard. If they regard the MNE entry as being purely based on export and that the export markets are not important to them, then the local firms will continue to produce to the local process standard. The degree of impact on the local firms is a function of the degree of competition the MNE represents for the local firms. In large economies where MNE entry is driven by a desire to capture local market share by driving up standards as a tool of competitive rivalry, this could be significant.

The case of product standards is largely similar to the case of process standards: local firms will only be forced to raise standards if the MNE targets their principal markets, i.e. local or export.

The case of service standards is, however, slightly different and potentially more interesting. Returning to our assumption of service standards being used as a tool of competitive rivalry, MNE entry in service sectors by definition is largely driven by a strategy to supply local markets.[17] In this case, increased competition from MNEs in local service sectors could force standards higher by virtue of the need for local competitors to respond to the increased competition. There is no issue of export and local markets for local firms so they cannot necessarily avoid foreign competition. The impact of MNE competition in this case could be significant: local firms could be forced to exit or be subject to takeover by the MNE. If MNEs use higher service standards as a tool of competitive rivalry they will also set 'best practice' measures for the local industry and future entrants, local or MNE, will be required to compete on those terms as a minimum for profitability.

3.5 Bringing the politics in to regulatory convergence

In order to bring regulatory convergence under these different scenarios into the analysis, it is necessary to assume that the MNE target country is seeking to align national regulatory standards with a multilateral or regional agreement.[18] In this case, the choice facing local rivals to the MNE is the same in the service standards and the process and product standards cases. The main difference between the service standard and the other two cases is the time it would take for the country to adopt and implement the new international standards. If the adoption and implementation process were reasonably fast, then local firms would need to respond quickly to the MNE entry fearing loss of market share. If the process were slower, then the local firms would be given breathing space to adjust to the future regulatory conditions.

Arguably, there is circularity in the argument here as MNE presence in a given scenario is likely to enhance the ability of states to adopt and implement new legislation. Indeed, the implications of the process of regulatory convergence on the structural adjustment in the sector will arguably vary depending on the degree of MNE involvement in the local sector. The political implications of this structural adjustment process will also be different subsequently.

If MNE involvement in the given local sector is significant, then the adjustment process to the new regulatory climate could be less costly as the MNE will have already brought expertise of operating under the new regulations. This means that economically efficient resources in the local sector will be reallocated, being employed by the MNE, and while the consequences of this structural adjustment will lead to unemployment, the reallocation within the industry should imply lower costs of retraining for factors in the industry. Politically, this reduces the pressure to resist the adjustment and would reduce the resources required to compensate losers from the changes.

Where MNE involvement in the sector is relatively low, a different result emerges. Domestic firms will be required to undertake the necessary changes within their production processes to meet the terms of new regulation and this could lead to a significantly longer adjustment process and higher costs in terms of resources in the industry being made redundant for a significant period.

What are the implications of this for the legislative and implementation process? It is useful to separate out two related issues. First, it is important to understand the political economy of regulatory convergence in the promulgation phase of new laws. Where local firms have derived their market position largely due to a specific national standard and have hitherto been sheltered from international competition, then it is likely there would be resistance to the introduction of new regulations. At a minimum, the local firms may seek to delay the introduction of legislation through national legislatures. Second, it is important to recognize the direct influence of the MNE in political lobbying for a given change in the legal and regulatory framework. In this instance, MNEs, seeking to exploit their competitive regulatory advantage, will attempt to hasten the introduction and implementation of standards that they have brought to the country as this directly imposes a cost on their competitors. Like the local firms, they would attempt to lobby legislators for these changes.

Thus if a direct policy objective of a government is to converge domestic rules and regulations with multilateral or regional accords, then the presence of MNEs producing to those standards will aid the legislative process. It is important to recognize that we assume that local firms' strategies are essentially inward-looking – eschewing an export strategy in order to preserve domestic market share. Political resources in lobbying are therefore invested in slowing down legislative change rather than speeding up the process.

3.6 Conclusions and implications

This finding is important because it allows us to reconsider the role of MNEs in their 'contribution' to economic and political development in domestic political economies. The critical developmental view of MNEs is that rather than promoting technology transfer and creating meaningful employment, MNEs seek to exploit local cost advantages (Cowling and Sugden 1987). Because the relative bargaining position of states in the developing world is weak, the MNE can further ignore environmental, social and political costs of their activities. The mainstream view of MNE activity is that they bring the necessary capital and knowledge to developing economies as well as raising living standards and creating employment. Accordingly, it is argued that local capital is insufficient to achieve these objectives and thus developing countries must have injections of foreign capital.

This chapter has demonstrated that under a set of assumptions, the MNE plays an additional regulatory enhancing role by raising process, product and service standards in economies seeking to adopt higher multilateral and regional regulatory frameworks. Given the increase in the scope and volume of multilateral rules and regimes in the last half century combined with the gradual, albeit patchy, shift from domestic to international governance, this chapter suggests that states wishing to participate in the world political economy may need to encourage further liberalization of their economies by bringing in MNEs.

Through the mechanisms outlined above, MNEs could considerably contribute to the process of regulatory convergence and reduce the time and cost impact of structural adjustment caused by the shift to the new regulatory framework.

It is vital, however, to recognize the caveats in this analysis and more importantly the limited scope of its application. First, this chapter, as with our book as a whole, does not attempt to offer a comprehensive panacea for development strategies for all domestic political economies in the world.[19] Second, this analysis can only be relevant where states are attempting to raise domestic standards to higher international ones. Third, the role of MNEs in this scenario is clearly sensitive to the strategy of the MNE itself. For example, if the MNE is not seeking to use the local economy as a basis for export growth but seeking to sell to the local market, it may adapt its product to the standards of the local market. Fourth, this chapter does not deal with the broader issues of the impact on the domestic economy of FDI.

The current EU enlargement process where transition political economies in East and Central Europe (ECE) are seeking to become members of the EU is an excellent 'testing ground' for the concepts in this chapter. This is because enlargement involves probably the most comprehensive process of regulatory convergence in the contemporary world political economy. It is also interesting because the participation of MNEs across the ECE region has been uneven, with some political economies such as Hungary and Poland receiving large amounts of FDI and others such as Slovenia, Bulgaria and Romania receiving comparatively lower levels. Other empirical material could be analysed in the case of NAFTA and regional integration in Mercosur.

For the discipline of IPE, while it is clear that an analysis of states remains central to an understanding of the politics of regulatory convergence, our chapter suggests that scholars may need to cast their analytical net wider and seek other non-state influences on regulatory convergence. Excellent work has already been accomplished in analysing the direct influence of firms in the European context (Kohler-Koch 1997; Middlemas 1995; Wallace and Young 1997). Hocking and McGuire (2001), Lawton and McGuire (2001) and Pigman (2001) have carried out similar research on international organizations and forums.

In a similar fashion, from the perspective of international business studies, the political impact of business strategy is clearly an increasingly important field of study as firms become increasingly important in international politics.

Our next chapter turns to the empirical setting for our research: East and Central Europe's economic transition process and the current phase of EU enlargement to incorporate these political economies.

4
The Empirical Setting: EU Enlargement and the Process of Regulatory Convergence

4.1 Introduction

In Chapters 2 and 3, we have set up our analytical and theoretical framework for examining the role of MNEs in the process of regulatory convergence. We have argued that both the IPE and IBS literatures have significantly aided our understanding of the important influence of the MNE in the world political economy. Based on these insights, we attempted a synthesis of the two literatures in Chapter 3 by focusing on how MNEs influence the process of regulatory convergence by using higher industrial standards as a tool of competitive rivalry. Taking Murphy's (1995) terminology, we called this regulatory competitive advantage. This was because we showed how an MNE could use its higher industrial standards to compete with domestic rivals. We suggested that exploitation of higher standards was especially salient in service industries where the main means of MNEs to differentiate themselves is to use higher service standards than the local firms. Indeed, quality of service (at a similar or lower price) is the hallmark of excellence in service sectors.

Where states are seeking to align their regulatory standards with other states or international agreements that have higher standards, under certain conditions, we argue that FDI and the presence of MNEs can facilitate this process. Indeed, the contemporary world political economy has witnessed a growth in regional and global economic integration agreements of varying breadth and reach. As a partial consequence of these arrangements, the growth of FDI as a percentage of world economic output has increased. Indeed, as the emphasis of the integration agreements has been to liberalize trade and investment, the increase in economic interdependence brought about by the activities of the MNE has added further impetus to the process of economic integration. This 'virtuous circle', we argue, continues to strengthen the role played by the MNE in facilitating further regulatory convergence.[1] As documented and analysed in the literature, the MNE influence is both direct (through lobbying and technocratic participation in international standard setting bodies) and, we argue, indirect, through the role of leveraging regulatory competitive advantage.

This chapter aims to examine this theoretical proposition empirically. In the current world political economy, there are a number of interesting and useful potential empirical cases to examine. These include Western hemispheric integration (NAFTA, Mercosur) and EU integration and enlargement to include states from ECE.

The process of economic integration in both North America (NAFTA) and in South America (Mercosur) is a tempting case to pursue. First, the role of US and other MNEs is extensive in the economic development of North and South America. Trade liberalization has proceeded at a rate faster than many would have expected given the chequered history of economic and political relations in the Western hemisphere.

The main drawback of exploring this process is that the integration itself remains limited to predominantly 'at the border' forms of integration. In particular, NAFTA specifies clearly that the agreement remains purely intergovernmental and does not directly cover areas of domestic regulation.

By contrast, the process of EU enlargement is considerably more far-reaching for the states seeking to join. As the EU itself is a highly integrated entity, based around microeconomic and macroeconomic policy integration (the Single Market and Economic and Monetary Union (EMU)), those states seeking to join (hereafter candidate countries) need to experience a process of approximation of laws hitherto not undertaken anywhere in the world political economy. As the process of EU integration has deepened, an increasing level of governmental resources has been required to promulgate and enforce EU policy norms.[2] In addition to this, EU membership has required important changes in governmental and business culture. Attitudes to regulation as it pertains to transparency in public services, health and safety in the workplace have, among others, revolutionized the rights of citizens and the obligations of governments and employers.

We organize this chapter as follows. In part two we examine the nature of EU integration and how it relates to regulatory convergence specifically. In part three we evaluate the position of the candidate countries in this process and in particular relate the process of economic transition, the arrival of FDI in the region and the process of enlargement. We argue that as the terms of economic transition from a socialist planned economy towards varying degrees and forms of market-based mixed economies has proceeded, the role of FDI has been crucial to the outcomes of transition. Moreover, we suggest that those candidate countries that have been open to FDI have benefited from this process.[3] Crucially, we hypothesize that those candidate countries that have higher levels of FDI will be more able to implement the necessary laws and practices that make up the *acquis communautaire* more effectively. Part four is a concluding section and takes us into our discussion of empirical methodology in Chapter 5.

4.2 EU integration and regulatory convergence: a brief narrative

At this stage, it is worthwhile undertaking a slight diversion in order to understand why EU integration is a good case for our theoretical claims. There is no unified and universally accepted theory of EU integration. Rather, it can be explained from a range of perspectives.[4] For the sake of tractability, there is an important contrast in the political science literature on the difference between supranational and intergovernmental explanations for EU integration. One school argues that EU integration represents a new, supranational phase in political integration where new actors and institutions are gaining sovereignty at the expense of states (e.g. Haas 1964; Hix 1999). Opposing this view is a school that argues the opposite: that EU integration is a grand bargain between states that agree to deepen cooperation, as it is their self-interest to do so (Moravscik 1998; Wallace and Young 1997). Whichever school is correct, the result of EU integration is that domestic regulation among the EU member states has become directly influenced by the creation of new EU-level regulations and policies.[5] This is what Lawrence et al. (1996) refer to as 'deep integration'. One of the core aims of the EU, as stated in the

Treaty of Rome, was to create a common market. The common market requires measures to create free movement of goods, services, capital and persons. Superficially, this aim implied a deregulatory set of measures, i.e. the removal of existing national standards. In the context of the political economy of EU integration, this suggested a relatively cost-free exercise. Moreover, it appealed to an increasingly popular belief in the efficacy of markets over states.[6]

However, as member states were to discover, once national regulations had been removed, there remained considerable issues about whether there should be EU-wide regulations.[7] Moreover, early attempts at harmonization of standards failed, as there was no agreement on a common standard. In response to this, member states agreed on a new approach: mutual recognition. This required that member states would respect each other's national standards and not use their own standard, wittingly or otherwise, to prevent the flow of the 'Four Freedoms'.[8] This process itself was started in the early 1980s when, under the EU Commission Presidency of Jacques Delors, the 1985 White Paper was drawn up.[9] This White Paper called for the introduction of around 350 measures to create the Single Market. It was a notable success for Delors. By 1986, member states had agreed to implement the recommendations and amended the Treaty of Rome through creation of the Single European Act (SEA). Far from being an exercise in dismantling national regulations, the SEA, as has been later recognized, was the most far-reaching exercise in regulatory reform in EU history. Not only did member states have to amend existing national laws to allow for liberalization but new regulatory cultures and practices had to be introduced (with varying degrees of effort and success).[10]

One of the most remarkable aspects of the process was that within six years of the process being launched, the EU proclaimed that on 1 January 1993, the Single Market was in place.[11] Indeed, one of the consequences of the success of the SEA was that it created further political momentum for the completion of EMU by 1999.[12]

Apart from the ideologically attractive nature of the SEA, a second reason for its success lay in the nature of politics at stake. While many international agreements are based around high politics – grand declarations of intent with little emerging action subsequently – the SEA was based on the politics of technocrats. This form of low politics – dealing with the byzantine details of food standards and electrical power tool voltages – allowed the role of EU bureaucrats and their national counterparts to drive the process well below the eyes of nationally elected politicians. In fact, a political process called 'comitology' was developed in the EU to facilitate the agreement of new legislation. This procedure was based on the principle that certain issues did not require high-level political agreement of member states and could therefore be delegated to technical committees staffed by member state appointees and EU Commission permanent staff.[13]

While the political legitimacy of this approach may be questionable, it has significantly speeded up the process of decision-making. Without it, it is arguable whether the EU could have achieved as much legislative progress as it has. These procedures are also very durable. The absence of an EU constitution, in the traditional state sense, means that once practices become embedded in an EU process, they are extremely difficult to alter.

While committees, far from the watchful gaze of national ministers and parliaments, went about creating the legislative framework for the SEA, they sought important advice about the appropriate regulatory policies. As the overriding view of the SEA was based on technocratic policy-making, EU bureaucrats went to industry to consult on the relevant structures and technicalities of the new legislation. This created a crucial influence for industry in the nature of new regulations. Groups in industry accepted the opportunity to act as advisers. The EU Commission called upon a range of experts, from committees to examine electricity standards (CENELEC) to ESPRIT committees.

One important group was the European Roundtable of Industrialists (ERT). This group consisted of senior executives in major European MNEs. Explicitly pushing a liberalization agenda, the ERT played a crucial role in influencing senior bureaucrats to see the need for EU action. The message sent by the ERT was simple, to quote Cowles: 'support the single market programme or European industry will invest elsewhere' (Cowles 1997: 130).[14]

To date, the SEA is recognized as the cornerstone of future attempts at integration. Most EU criteria for the success of integration refer back to the need for a functioning market economy. Member states of the European Free Trade Association (EFTA),[15] recognizing the rapid development of the EU Single Market, were soon to agree a special arrangement whereby they could participate in the Single Market through the European Economic Area (EEA) agreement. While gaining access for their industry and consumers, the member states had virtually no influence in the legislative and regulatory process in the Single Market.[16] Indeed, soon after acceding to the EEA, Austria, Finland, Norway and Sweden sought full membership of the EU. In a referendum in Norway, voters rejected the proposal to join whereas referendums were successful in the other three states.[17]

Part of the haste with which the Finnish and Swedish governments sought to gain full membership of the EU was explained by a fear that continuing outside could lead to a hollowing out of their economies. In the media in both Sweden and Finland, chairmen of large Swedish and Finnish MNEs such as Ericsson, Nokia, Neste and Electrolux threatened, in a manner similar to the ERT threat cited above, that failure to join the EU could lead them to move their activities to within the EU as this was where their main markets were.

Thus, it is important to emphasize the role of the European MNEs in influencing, driving and facilitating the process of EU integration. On both a direct and indirect political level MNEs were crucial in ensuring that EU-wide legislation would reflect the demands of industry. Moreover, in driving the standard setting process at an EU level, they created a double-sided phenomenon. On the one hand, the creation of a Single Market created a potentially larger market for MNEs, more consumers, and greater economies of scale and scope served to increase potential profitability. At the same time, the Single Market implied greater competition across borders, the threat of takeover, and rather less so, public procurement markets for some of Europe's largest corporations. Probably one of the unexpected consequences of the Single Market for MNEs was the increased activism and scrutiny of competition policy by the EU Commission.[18] EU competition policy both in the field of merger control but also prosecution of restrictive business practices has been significant in controlling anti-competitive conduct of MNEs in a range of sectors.

Thus the European MNE has played a central role in the development, advancement and evolution of EU rules on market conduct in a range of ways as described above. We now turn our discussion to a brief narrative of the process of economic and political transition in East and Central Europe.[19]

4.3 Economic transition in Central and East Europe and the MNE

While the EU was launching upon the most comprehensive policy step with the creation of the Single Market, monumental changes were occurring in East and Central Europe (ECE). The former state-planned political economies from Czechoslovakia to Ukraine collapsed and along with them the political system of one-party states led by socialist parties across the region. The year 1989 was remarkable for several reasons but most of all because few, if any, commentators on either side of the Iron Curtain had predicted the precipitous collapse of socialism. Led by the reformist Mikhail Gorbachev in the Soviet Union, in a matter of a few months, borders were opened to West Europe, the Berlin Wall had collapsed (literally and physically) and socialist leaders were thrown out of office. Less than two years later, Gorbachev would himself undergo the humbling experience of resigning while presiding over the dissolution of the Soviet Union.

4.3.1 Unpredictable changes and differing trajectories

With hindsight, it was hardly surprising that such incredible trans-formations in two years would have left EU member states and the US government floundering, unable to muster a policy response to these changes. The challenges facing all actors in the light of the collapse of the bi-polar Cold War were numerous and daunting. We shall cover the EU response to these changes in section 4.4 below. Here we focus more specifically on the question of the response to the collapse of the political economies and in what ways the new democ-ratic political economies of ECE developed a process of transition. In particular, we aim to demonstrate the role played by FDI and MNEs in the economic transition process and how their presence has configured the political landscape in the region.

However, it is important to note at this stage that, for several states in ECE, one of their most consistent foreign policy aims since the collapse of socialism in the region was accession to the EU. Policies of transition in this sense should be understood in this light. Indeed, as is noted below, there are quite remarkable similarities between the ideological emphasis among states in ECE towards concepts of societal and economic transformation and those of the EU.[20]

The rhetorical and ideological commitment to the market in some senses paved the way for the remarkable role played by MNEs in the economic development of ECE.

Once again, with hindsight, the solutions to the rapid collapse of state-planned political economies have evolved very much in line with the severe problems faced by the new leaders in ECE at the time. Moreover, a complex interaction between historical, geo-political, cultural and economic factors meant that it is hard to discern a clear pattern in the response to the transition process.[21] Thus, we can contrast the experience of the former GDR, which was fully absorbed by West Germany almost immediately, with the case of Moldova, which is still in the early phases of transition a decade after the collapse of the Soviet Union. We can also observe the disintegration of societies in ECE: the peaceful separation of the Czech Republic from Slovakia; the terrible, war-torn collapse and disintegration of Yugoslavia into almost mono-ethnic states. We can compare the success of small states such as Estonia who have moved rapidly to a market-based political economy with that of Europe's largest state, Russia, whose political and economic collapse appears to be intensifying rather than diminishing ten years after the collapse of the Soviet Union. Thus, the experience of ECE political economies has been remarkably varied despite virtually all states in the region proclaiming their commitment to the marketization of their respective societies.[22]

As pointed out by the United Nations Economic Council for Europe (UNECE) as early as 1993, the supposed dichotomy between gradualist and 'Shock Therapy' approaches to the transition process had not produced clear results. The implicit assumption behind this dichotomy was that states that pursued Shock Therapy would likely witness more success in transition whereas gradualist solutions would implicitly allow for discontent caused by the changes to lead to a stalling of the necessary reforms. Thus, the Shock Therapist Russian policy can be contrasted with the gradualist Slovenian strategy. Similarly, Poland's rapid transition process can be compared with the erratic progress made by the Bulgarian political economy. Perhaps the common link between all four of these political economies has been that Poland and Slovenia's proximity to the EU compared with Bulgaria, and its peripheral location in the war-torn Balkans and Russia, its land mass stretching from the Baltic Sea to the Pacific is more important in determining success.

4.3.2 The general features of ECE political economies before 1989

While the experience of ECE political economies has differed based around the speed of change, the sequencing of reforms and the broader structural differences discussed above, almost without exception, the main aim of the process, both on a rhetorical and actual basis has been to create a functioning market economy that is embedded in the world political economy.

It is therefore important to consider the state of planned political economies before 1989. Again, significant differences can be observed. Before we consider these, it is useful to posit the main characteristics of planned economies in the period leading to 1989. On a macroeconomic level, growth in output had slowed dramatically. While prices and therefore the rate of inflation had remained largely unchanged, this was hiding severe dislocations in resource allocation in the political economies. As capital flows into the region from outside were severely restricted, it was impossible to consider the true exchange rates (and hence purchasing power) of the currencies of these political economies. The macroeconomic performance of ECE political economies was arguably intimately related to the microeconomic distortions in these countries. First, labour and capital productivity was extremely low. This was related to the nature of state socialism itself where absenteeism from the workplace, grossly inadequate capital provision and an emphasis on physical value of output undermined performance.[23] Second, technology transfer, both within the region and from outside the region was negligible or inappropriate.[24] Third, the central political control of most forms of economic activity from the socialist party ensured that only changes that would reinforce the political power of the socialist *apparatchik* would be tolerated. Inherently, this bred a culture of political and economic conservatism that undermined enterprise. Fourth, as the most productive and advanced aspects of economic activity in most of the ECE political economies were allocated within the military-industrial complex, there was a severe shortage of consumer-based service provision. Fifth, as trade with West Europe and North America was highly restricted and controlled, the ability of new technological and entrepreneurial trends to be reflected in ECE was extremely limited.

While these five characteristic features of the ECE region before 1989 are general, we can note several important differences and particularities of some of the ECE political economies. Yugoslavia was arguably the more liberal of the planned political economies both domestically and internationally. Largely as a consequence of the foreign policy of Marshall Tito, which sought to distance the Yugoslav state from the Soviet Union, the Yugoslav economy was a significant recipient of foreign aid from West Europe and the USA. Domestically, highly limited forms of private entrepreneurship were tolerated. Greater political autonomy was granted to the future successor states of Yugoslavia, partly in a bid to implement the more liberal economy policy but also as an attempt to contain the ethnic 'powder keg' within Yugoslavia.

Hungary, the central feature of our study, also permitted limited forms of 'market socialism' whereby people were permitted to run small businesses, own private property and, within reason, travel abroad fairly easily.[25]

The experience of Hungary and Yugoslavia can be readily contrasted with the experience of two forms of extreme autarky: Romania and Albania. In both cases, there was an extreme attempt at national economic self-sufficiency combined with ruthless political control.[26]

The range of political economies such as Poland, Czechoslovakia and East Germany, partly because of their geo-strategic position close to Germany and the NATO alliance, meant that control of these political economies was heavily influenced directly by the Socialist Party of the Soviet Union.[27] The Baltic states, Estonia, Lithuania and Latvia, were of course part of the Soviet Union.

Thus while we are able to draw general similarities, it is important to remember that in 1989, when the transition process started, all the ECE political economies were starting off from their own specific experiences.

4.3.3 Steps towards market economies[28]

The transition to a market political economy for ECE was unique especially because the policy advisers to the governments of the region were expecting them to develop institutions and practices that have taken decades, if not centuries, for other political economies elsewhere in the world to develop. Clearly, while institutional learning would significantly aid in the development of blueprints, the task was still substantial. In what may probably become one of the seminal, and the most controversial, pieces of political economy in the past half century, Sachs (1994) stated that a transition political economy needs to take four steps in order to move towards a successful market economy: domestic price liberalization, privatization, trade and monetary liberalization. Moreover, these steps should be taken quickly in order to ensure the necessary 'shock' to the emerging market economy is sufficiently strong, i.e. in order to prevent a return to socialist structures. Each of these steps was substantial and far-reaching and required significant changes to other areas of government policy such as fiscal policy and the role of the welfare state. In particular, the policy proposals suggested that the state, and its level of spending, would have to shrink drastically.[29] While not every political economy in the region implemented the changes in the order and speed with which Sachs suggested, these four steps were central to all programmes of reform in the region.

While this had huge implications for public financial and macroeconomic management by the architects of the new political economies in ECE, we are interested in one of the central implications of the transition: the significantly increased role for foreign capital in the region.[30] Not only did trade and monetary liberalization increase the influence of international prices and general economic trends, privatization of state-owned enterprises, if carried out in a certain way, would substantially enhance the role of foreign ownership of domestic industry.[31]

At the time, there was a significant debate about the privatization process related to the trade-off between equity and efficiency. While, arguably, foreign sales of state enterprises would lead to significant cost efficiencies in the short term, it was unlikely to lead to the 'enterprise-ownership' culture that was a central aim of the reforms. To an extent share voucher schemes could go some way to achieving that but may imply a slower process of restructuring of enterprises as owners, i.e. citizens and employees of the enterprises, may resist changes.[32]

Another problem facing the privatization authorities was how to actually value state enterprises even before sales to foreigners could take place. Clearly in market value terms, it would be difficult to sell capital assets that by West European and US standards were close to zero. Moreover, the political ramifications of 'cherry picking' of state assets by foreigners could be huge.[33]

However, perhaps the largest problem facing a number of the states in ECE was a huge foreign debt problem. In order to maintain declining living standards in the region, governments borrowed heavily from abroad from a range of international organizations and foreign governments.[34] Thus rather than exacting and theoretically sound arguments from economic advisers about the need for foreign competition to enhance efficiency, the basic dilemma of indebtedness forced the hands of many governments in the region.

The process that the various ECE political economies took is complex and highly differentiated, and is therefore out of the scope of our study. The work of Bruszt and Stark (1999) is a detailed and comprehensive analysis of this process.[35] As of writing, the situation of some ECE political economies appears to be good with a general mood of optimism for the future.[36] However, the seemingly intractable problems facing Russia and other successor states appear daunting. Moreover, as it seems unlikely that they will be invited to participate in negotiations for EU membership in the near future, a centrifugal force could emerge whereby political economies that remain outside of the EU negotiating framework will find themselves further away from an enlarged West and Central European core of states within the EU.

4.4 The European Union response to the changes in Central and East Europe

As argued above, the response of the EU member states to the dramatic changes in 1989 was understandably piecemeal and haphazard. As Sedelmeier and Wallace (2000: 355) put it: 'There was no choice possible other than hyperactivity and speed and no opportunity to relate short-term action to crafted future goals. Policymakers had to work from imperfect analogues and from more or less good intention. The result was a curious mix of tradition and innovation.'

The initial ad hoc policies consisted of quickly signing trade and cooperation agreements on a bilateral basis with ECE governments. These trade agreements committed the EU to progressively lifting all quantitative restrictions on trade except in a number of 'sensitive' sectors such as steel, textiles and agriculture.

A second 'leg' of the immediate policy response to 1989 was to set up the PHARE (Poland and Hungary: Aid for the Restructuring of

Economies – later extended to other countries). The European Bank for Reconstruction and Development (EBRD) was also set up as a broader initiative and based largely on a private sector basis. Loans made available through the EBRD were governed by commercial loan principles. The US government at the time was keen to see the EU as leading the process of support for the ECE political economies and for it to take somewhat of a backseat in the organization and implementation of the aid and support packages (Sedelmeier and Wallace 2000: 357).

We can thus see immediate differences between the policy of the US government after World War Two *vis-à-vis* West Europe and that taken by the Bush administration after 1989. While both ideological considerations and *realpolitik* in a Cold War context largely helped to explain US post-World War Two generosity towards West Europe in the form of Marshall Aid, no such generosity was extended to the new post-socialist governments in 1989.

As economic recession and a new ideological emphasis underplaying the role of the state in economic management had taken hold in most industrialized political economies, the role of aid was to be indicative and based around the creation of markets rather than new political and economic institutions. The EU member states' response was, in the early stages at least, typified by this approach.

The PHARE programme was administered by the EU Commission as agreed by member states. The Commission set up a new agency within its Directorate-General for External Relations (then DG-1) and its staff were responsible for monitoring the agreed plans between the EU Commission and the ECE governments. Several initial problems emerged. First, overall cost structures were heavily weighted in favour of the plethora of West European 'consultants' hired by the PHARE staff to aid in the appraisal and implementation of projects. Arguably, the resources that were intended for the ECE political economies were not reaching their target. Second, the problems of 'absorption' of the funds became significant. This was because the state bureaucracies in ECE political economies were not able to handle the resources that were available under the PHARE projects. Third, other Directorates-General in the EU Commission began to set up their own projects with ECE countries thus adding to the impression of an uncoordinated approach to the events of 1989.

The EBRD was a broader, pan-European initiative based around the idea of providing public funds for directly productive purposes in the ECE political economies. In some limited sense, the EBRD, by building around principles of finance capital, was similar to the World Bank and IFC approaches to development aid. It is independent of the EU and thus operates on a completely separate basis from the EU institutions.

4.4.1 The Europe Agreements

Soon after the initial phase, the EU member states agreed to set up a process of 'association' for ECE states with the EU. The Europe Agreements as they were called were a more comprehensive package of measures than earlier trade and cooperation agreements. They were unlimited in duration and created, for the first time, institutionalized political dialogue. The main institution was the Association Council that was set to meet at ministerial level at least once a year. Its role was to supervise the Europe Agreements' implementation. The main areas covered by the agreements were provisions for the free movement of goods to allow for the free trade in industrial goods within five years for EU members states and ten years for ECE signatories; progressive but highly restricted movement of persons and right of establishment; and approximation of legislation of ECE associates with EU laws.

The first ECE states to enter into negotiations under the Europe Agreements were Czechoslovakia, Hungary and Poland in 1990. The Association recipe very much reflected the traditional approach of EU integration based around limited and progressive institutional and policy-making harmonization. At this point, there was no clear public statement that ECE political economies were to be invited to join the EU.

4.4.2 The accession process

It was not until the mid-1990s that the EU member states had formulated a comprehensive approach towards their relations with ECE transition political economies. While a significant amount of polemic was expressed about the dangers of enlarging the EU and an equally large degree of claims from ECE that the EU was not serious about enlargement, the member states agreed at the Copenhagen Summit in June 1993 to begin a process of accession for ECE states to join the EU. As expressly stated by the member states at the Copenhagen European Council, it was not a matter of whether ECE states would be welcomed into the EU but rather a matter of when it would occur.

Thus, accession would be based on a set of criteria (hereafter the Copenhagen Criteria) that were broad and encompassed both political and economic elements. We shall return in more detail to the question of economic criteria, but it is worth mentioning here that the political criteria were an important precondition for successful accession for candidate countries. This is because given the new emerging political institutions in the ECE region, member states were keen to emphasize that actual, practical adherence to democratic institutions and the protection of minorities and human rights were important conditions of membership.[37] Put more bluntly, EU member states wished to emphasize the complete incompatibility of pre-1989 political institutions in ECE with those of the EU.

The economic criteria were, in some senses, part of the transition that was already taking place in the region. These were the existence of a functioning market economy as well as the capacity to cope with competitive pressure and market forces within the Union, and the ability to take on the obligations of membership including adherence to the aims of political, economic and monetary union. Indeed, most countries' main foreign economic policy objective has been EU membership. In this sense, EU membership provided a useful 'endgame' for the process of market liberalization.[38] Once they had achieved EU membership, it could be rightly claimed that they were 'functioning market (political) economies'. However, in addition to these important and far-reaching criteria, ECE political economies would need to ensure that they had created the conditions for their integration through the adjustment of administrative structures, so that European Community legislation transposed into national legislation is implemented effectively through appropriate administrative and judicial structures. This relates to the need to implement the *acquis communautaire* fully.

In this context, it is important that implementation did not simply relate to the introduction of laws into the statutes of ECE states. The EU member states were keen to ensure that the EU regulations and directives were being actually implemented. This has been carried out through an extensive set of EU Commission teams who have been sent out to the region to verify that implementation is being carried out effectively.[39]

Indeed, the concept of effective implementation has entered the discourse of the EU negotiators.[40] It is unlikely that accession for any of the candidate countries will take place before effective implementation is achieved. Moreover, as citizens in candidate countries begin to develop an awareness of their economic and political rights offered by EU membership, states in candidate countries could find themselves challenged at the European Court of Justice for failure to effectively resource and enforce the EU *acquis*.

This is where one of the central claims of this book has an important resonance: if MNEs raise the standards used in sectors subject to EU regulation, the costs of effective implementation and convergence towards the new standards will likely be lower. This is because the use of standards as a competitive weapon will facilitate the adjustment process faced by these sectors. This has two effects. First, political resistance to the introduction of new legislation will be reduced, as foreign companies are likely to have acquired an important share of the market. We shall demonstrate this effect in later chapters when we explore the Hungarian cases. Both foreign rivals and local companies used higher standards as their principal strategic survival strategy. Second, administrative resources required to implement new standards will be lower because the standards will already be in force in the sector. In other words, standards will be raised by competitive rivalry prior to legislative change.

The decisions of the Copenhagen European Council were further reinforced by the Essen European Council agreements that set up a 'pre-accession strategy' for the EU and ECE states. In particular, the economic substance of the Europe Agreements was to be superseded by the decision to prepare ECE political economies to integrate into the internal market. This required the phased adoption of legislation and regulations that were compatible with EU rules. The Essen decisions also brought the ECE states into cooperative structures concerning trans-European networks (TENs), participation in Justice and Home Affairs (JHA), culture, education and training. Following the Essen European Council, the EU Commission prepared a White Paper on bringing the ECE political economies into the internal market in May 1995 and presented it to member states at the Cannes European Council a month later.

The rapid development of an EU policy towards the ECE states ensured that three years after the 1995 White Paper was presented, the process of accession negotiations had begun and the monumental task of bringing ECE laws into conformity with the *acquis communautaire* had also begun. Following the start of negotiations, a pressing issue needed to be addressed by the EU member states. This was the future financing of the EU in the light of the end of the 1993–9 budgetary cycle and in anticipating the costs of EU enlargement in budgetary terms. The proposals were forwarded in a Commission document entitled Agenda 2000. This document argued for the largest ever amount of EU funds to be put forward for the process of enlargement and sought to simplify existing EU rules on regional support in order to accommodate the candidate countries. The member states accepted the document and this has been the financial basis for EU enlargement. However, two key issues remained outstanding at the time of writing.

First, member states had still not agreed on reform of the Common Agricultural Policy. This was because existing member states such as France and Germany did not wish to extend the same degree of financial support to the farmers of the candidate countries as compared with the agricultural sectors of the existing member states. Extending support would require a substantial increase in budgetary allocations as well as a net redistribution of funds from member states' farming communities towards their poorer ECE counterparts. Second, free movement of persons from the candidate countries (upon accession) to the rest of the EU will not be on the basis of the 1986 SEA 'Four Freedoms'. Fearing political opposition to large-scale migration East to West, current member states have demanded a seven-year transition period in which free movement of persons from ECE candidates to the EU-15 will be limited. After the first seven-year period, the policy will be reviewed with no presumption that it will be automatically lifted.

We now turn our attention to our case study: Hungary. We begin by examining FDI trends in Hungary as a basis for linking the role of MNEs in Hungary and the process of regulatory convergence.

4.5 FDI in Hungary

Having discussed the accession process facing the current candidate countries, we now turn our attention to an understanding of the impact of FDI in Hungary. Table 4.1 outlines the proportions of

Table 4.1   FDI in ECE by recipient countries in percentage terms

Country	1990	1995	1998	1999
Albania	–	0.6	0.5	0.4
Belarus	–	0.1	0.6	0.7
Bulgaria	0.1	0.9	1.8	2.2
Czech Republic	45.5	20.2	17.1	15.8
Estonia	–	2.0	2.2	2.4
Hungary	19.0	27.5	18.8	18.6
Latvia	–	1.7	1.9	1.8
Lithuania	3.2	1.0	1.9	2.0
Moldova	–	0.3	0.3	0.3
Poland	3.6	21.6	26.7	29.2
Romania	25.6	3.2	5.2	5.3
Russia	–	15.0	16.8	16.1
Slovakia	2.9	3.4	3.0	2.0
Ukraine	–	2.5	3.3	3.2
Total	100.0	100.0	100.0	100.0

Source: World Investment Report, United Nations, 2000.

inward FDI in various ECE political economies. The figures are percentages of the total FDI stock to the region. As can be readily noted from the data, Hungary has maintained a steady share of the total FDI stock of around 20 per cent alongside Poland, the leading recipient, and the Czech Republic. Russia also has a relatively important share of around 15 per cent of the total. However, in per capita terms, it is trivial given Russia's large population. By comparison, in per capita US$ terms, in 1999 Hungary had the highest per capita FDI at $1896/capita, the Czech Republic was second with $1580/capita. Poland is third with only $775/capita.[41]

Hungary's position as one of the leading recipients of FDI is undisputable and it is important to note that, in 1999, 40 per cent of total company assets in Hungary were owned by foreign investors; 50 per cent of total gross industrial value-added and 57 per cent of investment were performed with foreign capital. Lastly, 76 per cent of imports and 80 per cent of exports were carried out by MNEs in Hungary.[42] FDI in Hungary employs around a quarter of the Hungarian workforce.[43] Despite the phasing out of most foreign investment incentives, a stable and favourable business environment and a large skilled workforce continued to attract a robust flow of FDI, increasingly into capital- and skill-intensive sectors. Net FDI inflows amounted to 2.1 billion in 2000 and a similar performance is expected in 2001. In recent years, most of the inflows have represented Greenfield investment, as the privatization process has neared completion, and only a very few large enterprises are left for sale.[44]

More than 18 000 joint ventures are registered in Hungary with thirty-five of the fifty top MNEs in the world economy having subsidiaries in Hungary.[45] Many MNEs regard Hungary as a 'hub' of their ECE operations with over eighty MNEs having their regional headquarters based in Hungary.[46]

FDI in total manufacturing investment has been significantly above 50 per cent across most sectors of manufacturing. Among service industries, financial services show a strong role of FDI in total investment. This can be contrasted with agriculture where FDI as a percentage of total investment is somewhat lower.

This trend is somewhat supported by data on the level of FDI per company size in Table 4.2 There is a strong positive relationship between company size and amount of FDI. In Meskó (2001), the author finds that among SMEs, around 80 per cent of the total number of firms in Hungarian industry, only 17 per cent of the total FDI stock had been invested in these companies whereas over 50 per cent of FDI had been invested in companies employing more than 250 workers.

If we consider three variables to measure the contribution of FDI to the Hungarian economy – value added, net sales and investment – Meskó's data reveals a strong role for FDI in the Hungarian industry in Table 4.3 MNEs have contributed a growing rate of value added to

Table 4.2 Enterprises with foreign holding by company size, 1999

Size	Enterprises		FDI	
	Number	*Distribution* (%)	*Billion HUF*	*Distribution* (%)
0–9 persons	22,044	83	436	17
10–49	2750	10	269.7	10
50–249	1255	5	546.2	21
250+	384	2	1372.6	52
Total	26,433	100	2624.5	100

Source: Meskó (2001).

Table 4.3   Value added, net sales and investment in Hungary (1992–99) (billion HUF)

Year	Total	Value Added		Net Sales		Investment
		MNE	Total	MNE	Total	MNE
1992	1284.1	259.4	5761.5	1409.9	447.6	99.2
1993	1474.9	447.5	6558.9	2104.9	385.2	169.0
1994	1868.0	732.2	8405.9	3173.0	524.1	249.7
1995	2586.2	999.3	11697.1	4756.4	674.8	374.2
1996	3169.8	1354.2	14892.4	6572.5	884.5	455.9
1997	4089.6	2009.1	18992.1	9117.4	1119.2	644.7
1998	4958.2	2436.1	23480.0	11323.8	1428.8	817.7
1999	5531.4	2734.7	27089.8	13552.5	1675.2	952.4

Source: Adapted from Meskó (2001).

Table 4.4   Foreign trade and the contribution of MNEs in Hungary (1994–99) (billion HUF)

Year	Imports		Exports		Balance	
	Total	MNE %	Total	MNE %	Total	MNE %
1994	1537.0	57	1128.7	54	−408.3	65
1995	1936.4	63	1622.0	58	−314.4	89
1996	2763.9	70	2392.3	69	−371.6	81
1997	3961.2	74	3566.8	75	−394.4	63
1998	5511.5	74	4934.5	77	−577.0	49
1999	6645.6	76	5938.5	80	−707.1	47

Source: Meskó (2001).

Hungarian industry stabilizing at around half of the total value added. A similar picture emerges for sales where MNEs have increased their share from around a quarter of total industry sales to around 50 per cent by 1999. Investment growth has been of similar magnitude over the same period.

If we consider the foreign trade balance and MNEs, we can see that MNEs have been largely responsible for Hungary's trade openness especially *vis-à-vis* the EU. In Table 4.4 we can see that MNEs have contributed three-quarters of total imports since 1997 and even

Table 4.5 Exports and imports by country of origin (1998 and 1999) in percentage terms

Country	1998		1999	
	Imports	*Exports*	*Imports*	*Exports*
Germany	29.4	37.6	30.1	39.0
Netherlands	2.3	5.3	2.4	5.8
USA	3.9	5.1	3.3	5.9
Austria	10.5	9.8	9.4	8.4
UK	3.4	4.0	3.0	5.0
France	4.6	3.6	4.4	4.5
Italy	6.4	5.2	6.8	5.4
Switzerland	1.6	1.2	1.5	1.2
Belgium	2.0	2.9	2.3	3.4
Japan	4.1	0.3	4.4	0.3
Other	31.8	25.0	32.3	21.1
Total	100.0	100.0	100.0	100.0

Source: Meskó (2001).

more exports over the same period. While Meskó does not provide a breakdown of these trade flows by intermediate and finished product categories, MNE theory would suggest that a significant amount of this trade emanating from MNEs is of an intra-firm variety – especially imports where parts for assembly in Hungary have been an important feature of MNE activity in Hungary.

Table 4.5 breaks down foreign trade flows by country for the years 1998 and 1999. What is striking from the data is Hungary's bilateral trade with Germany which is the single biggest bilateral trade flow over the period considered. This is in line with both macroeconomic explanations and with the fact that German companies are the largest source of inward FDI in Hungary. Austria's geographical proximity and historical relationship with Hungary probably accounts for its second place in the data. Overall, the majority of Hungarian trade, as would be expected, is with the EU-15.

If we consider the regional distribution of FDI in Hungary, a centralized picture of MNE economic activity emerges. The Budapest–Szekesfehervar region (called Central Hungary) has received the majority of FDI from all countries of origin. The Great Plain (both northern and southern) has received significantly less FDI, further reinforcing its

Table 4.6   Regional distribution of FDI by countries of origin in percentage terms

Region	Germany	Netherlands	Austria	USA	France	Italy	Total
Central Hungary	63.5	67.6	74.0	56.7	53.0	57.3	66.5
Central Transdanubia	3.3	8.1	5.1	20.5	4.6	8.6	6.8
Western Transdanubia	10.0	11.9	13.5	4.2	14.0	6.2	9.0
Southern Transdanubia	3.0	0.9	3.5	0.0	0.4	1.4	2.0
Northern Hungary	10.1	6.8	31.4	4.6	4.0	4.5	6.7
Northern Great Plain	7.9	2.4	0.9	4.3	1.6	18.9	4.4
Southern Great Plain	2.2	2.3	1.6	9.7	22.4	3.1	4.6
Total	100.0	100.0	100.0	100.0	100.0	100.0	100.0

Source: Meskó (2001).

relative economic backwardness since 1989. The figures are given in Table 4.6.

The above data illustrate in stark terms the importance of FDI to the Hungarian economy, in being responsible for the majority of value added, the vast majority of foreign trade and for being an important source of employment and sales in the Hungarian economy. We would now like to consider another aspect of the impact of FDI: its role in facilitating regulatory change in Hungary in conformity with the *acquis communautaire*. Before we turn to this issue in our case studies in Chapters 6 through 8, we will outline Hungarian public policy incentives for FDI.

4.6 Public policy and FDI

The Hungarian state has used a range of incentives to attract FDI to the country. Notable among them is the 1988 Act on Investments of Foreigners in Hungary. The law provides a ten-year 100 per cent corporate tax holiday for all investments over $3 billion forint in certain underdeveloped regions in east Hungary and more than $10 billion forint elsewhere. The tax exemption lasts until 2011 and the current corporate tax rate is 18 per cent. This law is further supported by a range of other incentives including tax-free export zones, subsidies for export promotion activities and employment subsidies for companies employing large numbers of workers.

The emphasis on public policy for FDI has been to encourage the development of industrial parks. While there are over 100 of these parks, the largest seven parks in west Hungary account for over 80 per cent of total output. As the growth of FDI in west Hungary and Budapest has substantially outstripped that of the eastern counties of Hungary, one of the main aims of public policy in FDI is to attract more investment to the east. As we discuss in Chapter 6 on banking, there is a shortage of skilled labour in west Hungary as it has been difficult for workers to migrate from the east. Thus with the current EU enlargement process in train, Hungary is now eligible for significant amounts of pre-accession aid under the PHARE programme. This aid is being directed towards eastern counties of Hungary and this has been accompanied by an eastward shift of FDI. Whether the FDI will continue its movement further east and into neighbouring Yugoslavia and Ukraine remains to be seen. The removal of tax exemptions as dictated by EU accession may significantly impact on the attractiveness of Hungary as a location for FDI for resource-seeking purposes.[47] For market-serving FDI purposes, Hungary is likely to remain a highly attractive location in terms of the domestic market and as a regional hub.

4.7 Summary

In this chapter, we have attempted to give the reader a background in the empirical issues we deal with in the coming chapters. First, we have briefly covered the process of regulatory convergence in the EU in its historical context in order to give the reader a background in the 'politics' of the issue. One of the remarkable successes of EU integration has been the ability of member states to agree to 'low politics' as a vehicle for integration. It has generated a whole area of policy-making related to technocratic standards and rule setting. Second, we sketched a picture of the main dilemmas, challenges and responses of ECE political economies after 1989. While initial policy prescriptions centred around a debate over the speed with which reforms should take place, what has emerged in subsequent years is a realization that initial starting points and geo-economic location are also as (if not more) important than the speed of reforms. This meant that ECE political economies took different trajectories towards the creation of stable market economies – and with differing degrees of success. Third, we offered a short historical narrative on the development of EU policy towards ECE states. What has emerged from the EU member states has been an initially ad hoc approach eventually strengthened by a concerted attempt to incorporate new member states through a pre-accession strategy and accession negotiations themselves. Last, but not least, we set out some data on the role of FDI in Hungary in order to prepare the reader for our case studies in Chapters 6 to 8.

As we have argued in Chapters 2 and 3, the conceptual relevance of the role of FDI is strong, as evidenced by the existing literature on the issue as well as by our stylized conceptual model that we outlined in Chapter 3. So the next aim of our analysis is to present the results of our empirical study into the issue.

We have chosen to consider three sectors for our study on Hungary. These sectors are banking, electricity and telecommunications. The choice of these three sectors is explained in more detail in the next chapter where we turn to the methodology and empirical approach we have taken.

5
Case Study Methodology

5.1 Introduction

From the outset of this chapter, we are at pains to stress that the issues we are addressing in our study do not seek to explain everything. We are not claiming that the consequences of MNE behaviour that we explore here are replicated in all instances. As we argued in Chapter 3, the role of the MNE in raising regulatory standards appears to work under certain conditions. What we do argue, however, is that as there appears to be a trend towards increasing integration of regulatory systems on a regional basis, and to a lesser degree on a global basis the role of MNEs could be important in driving and furthering this process. This chapter aims to develop more explicitly our empirical methodology. In particular, by generating our empirical hypotheses and relating these to the case studies we develop, our aim is to build a framework, which we use in our case studies in the chapters that follow.

The chapter is organized as follows. Part one is a discussion of our hypotheses. We do not set up formalized hypotheses. Instead we rely on descriptive and discursive methods. Part two examines the case study method we have adopted to analyse our hypotheses. Part three is a discussion of the empirical material we are using as the basis of our research including an evaluation of the kinds of data we are using for our study.

5.2 Hypotheses

Any study of this empirical type needs to be grounded in some form of testable proposition. While our work does not aim to be comprehensive in explaining all cases and phenomena, we nevertheless regard it as important to have a set of guidelines within which to set out our study. As discussed in Chapter 2, our theoretical approach claims that where a MNE uses higher standards as a tool of competitive advantage, or out of necessity borne of its export strategy to markets where higher standards are required, this process can lead to an upgrading of industry standards in the political economies where the MNE invests. From the extensive MNE literature on the motives for MNE activity, Birkinshaw and Hood (1998) differentiated between market-serving and resource-seeking FDI. For the purposes of our research, this is a useful division. In Table 5.1 we develop a simple matrix of FDI motives divided by service and manufacturing and by size of host economy.

From this table, we can develop simple strategies for FDI. In large economies, both manufacturing and service sector activity can be driven by a need to service a local market and by a desire to access key resources available to the MNE in these sectors. Thus, for example, the USA has both a large domestic market in services and manufacturing and possesses key resources that are attractive to MNEs such as skilled labour. Both high-quality resources and high consumer income drive FDI. The incentives for FDI are therefore strong. A similar case could be made for developing economies such as China and India. However, we would need to be careful about the nature of the market-serving activities. India may possess an unusually high level of trained software engineers for manufacturing FDI and it may become an important centre for international call facilities. However, the low income levels among consumers means that market-serving FDI is different from the US case. In both India and China, FDI is based on low cost resource and low consumer income.[1]

Table 5.1   FDI motives by sector and economy matrix

	Service sector	*Manufacturing sector*
Large economy	Market serving – strong Resource seeking – strong	Market serving – strong Resource seeking – strong
Small economy	Market serving – strong Resource seeking – weak	Market serving – weak Resource seeking – strong

Source: Author's own.

For small economies, FDI motives are mixed in the Birkinshaw and Hood division. In the service sector, it is unlikely that small economies offer specific resources for the attraction of FDI, but almost by definition, the provision of services requires a local presence in most of these sectors. An exception to the resource-seeking case for small countries is Switzerland where the presence of a particular set of factor conditions in the watch industry, financial services or the pharmaceutical sector lends it a niche position. The manufacturing sector by contrast could be depicted as being attractive to FDI because of access to key resources which are used to produce products for re-export. An excellent case of this is Ireland, which has become the production hub for a significant number of US MNEs, who then sell into other markets in the EU.

As the small economy has a relatively small market to sell to, the market-serving motives for FDI in manufacturing are weak (although again, an exception would be highest income, small political economies such as Switzerland). An alternative strategy for MNEs would be to produce in one country for export to several countries on a regional basis. This is the case, for example, with GE Lighting based in Hungary which uses this base as its European production headquarters.[2] Thus, the country where the product was manufactured would be served, but on a regional basis along with neighbouring economies.[3] The motives for FDI would thus be resource-seeking rather than market-serving. Arguably, the main motive for manufacturing FDI in small economies would be resource-seeking presumably to be re-exported to other countries.

5.2.1 The relationship between FDI and regulatory convergence again

As we discussed in Chapter 3, where a political economy is in the process of undertaking to implement new regulatory standards, there are theoretical arguments to support the view that the presence of FDI can actually enhance this process. This is for two reasons. First, if these standards are based on higher international standards that are required for MNEs to sell in other markets, the FDI will produce to these standards. Second, if FDI is used to increase market share through market-serving motives, then MNEs may use higher standards as a tool of competitive rivalry.

Given these two propositions, we can apply them to our small/large country dichotomy. First, both large and small economies can benefit from the competitive rivalry argument as FDI in service sectors is driven by market-serving motives in both cases. Second, both large and small economies can benefit from the higher standard requirements for export. It is likely that the competitive rivalry argument would be stronger in large economies simply by virtue of the larger market being an attractive source for MNEs. This does not, however, undermine the case for small economies.

If a government is seeking to raise the regulatory standards in an industry, one means of doing so would be to encourage foreign companies to serve the local market based on higher international standards. This is arguably preferable to requiring local firms to meet higher standards as the adjustment process is likely to be longer for these companies and the political resistance to new standards from within the industry may slow down the process of introduction. In Chapter 6, focusing on the Hungarian energy sector, our interviews with both governmental, regulatory and industry managers illustrated the resistance among Hungarian parliamentarians to the introduction of new Electricity Acts which were based on EU energy directives.

5.3 Case studies

We now consider the case studies chosen for this book. At the outset, it is important to consider how we went about choosing our studies. Our basic approach was to focus on the service sector in Hungary as the empirical vehicle for our work. This was for three reasons. First, the service sector has experienced extensive foreign ownership of industry in Hungary. This allows us to explore how foreign ownership has contributed to convergence of Hungarian service standards towards EU ones. Second, some of the most important regulatory issues facing Hungary are in the service sectors where EU liberalization has not been based exclusively on the basis of mutual recognition but on the development of minimum standards. Third, in the service sectors we analyse, there are well-established regulatory bodies that are responsible for managing new regulatory systems.[4]

A fourth additional but general methodological reason for choosing services is that competitive rivalry in service standards is the main form of competition, whereas competition in product markets can be based on several strategic variables such as product differentiation and branding in addition to product standards. While in services competition, price is an important aspect of strategy, a central and attractive means of differentiating a firm from its rivals is to offer superior service provision (for a given cost). While MNE entry in product markets such as consumer goods can involve the introduction of higher standard products, they can also use 'lower' quality products, at lower price, as a form of competitive strategy. This is especially important when we are considering MNE entry into transition economies where income levels are not sufficiently high to allow for higher price products to enter the market successfully initially. In the service sector, it is less likely that lower price, lower quality standards will be used as a competitive strategy by MNEs. Indeed, one of the central commercial claims of MNEs is their ability to serve local clients and other MNEs based in the country better than their domestic rivals.[5]

A smaller but nevertheless relevant issue is that in the service sector, transition political economies have started from a very small service base. In other words, before the process of transition started, service sectors were relatively underdeveloped when compared with sectors elsewhere in the industrialized world. Thus, the 'service provision gap' between local companies and MNEs would likely be significant at the start of the transition process and may remain for a considerable period after MNE entry.

On this basis, we have selected three sectors in Hungary. These are the banking, electricity and telecommunications services sectors. In each of these sectors, MNE ownership of industry is considerable, with the average above 50 per cent of total industry control in all three sectors. Each of these three sectors is regulated by independent regulatory bodies in Hungary: the Financial Services Supervisory Authority, the Hungarian Energy Office and the Communication Authority of Hungary, respectively. All three sectors have well-defined regulatory standards that upon EU membership would need to be compliant with EU directives on liberalization and standards. Essentially in all three cases, competitive structures will have to be in place in order for EU accession to go ahead successfully.

From the perspective of the regulatory authorities, the role of foreign companies in this context is thought to be of crucial importance in facilitating adjustment of the sectors and driving up standards in these sectors. Thus, foreign companies serve an important political objective in allowing the Hungarian state to achieve its political ambitions of acceding to the EU. MNEs can also be used as an important lever in forcing change in industry. They allow states to use MNE 'best practice' as a political weapon in coercing opposition to structural adjustment. By linking this with EU membership, they can point to international necessity for change in order to pursue their agendas.

5.4 Case study material

We have attempted to use a combination of both primary and secondary material in our empirical research. Secondary material has been used as both explanatory and indicative material in our research. The types of secondary material we have used are broad, ranging from other empirical research in the sectors concerned on different topics, to published data and newspaper reports. We have been fortunate in that Hungary's position as one of the leading candidate countries has meant that there is a substantial secondary empirical literature. Moreover, Hungary's position as the leading per capita recipient of FDI in the ECE region has ensured that foreign language sources (especially in English) have enabled us to consider sectors that in other transition political economies are not as open to FDI, and consequently there is a relative paucity of secondary empirical material in English.

Our primary research methodology has been informed by two basic constraints. First, certain kinds of industry data are commercially sensitive material and therefore both companies and regulators have been unwilling to allow us to reproduce named material for this study. Where this has occurred, we have protected the identity of our sources or inferred from the original and confidential data. Second, we rely upon the comments of interviewees on the basis of our research questionnaire, assuming that the interviewees are not attempting to provide false information. Indeed, if the interviewees were deliberately seeking to mislead us, there is little we can do except to infer this. This takes us 'one step back' from our primary data. The majority of our interviews were carried out in English, but some of them were in Hungarian. Where this was the case, we made use of interpreters during the interviews. We are thus relying upon the accuracy of their interpretations. No interviews in Hungarian were carried out without us in attendance.

We interviewed both governmental and industry managers for our research. We had two different questionnaires. First, the governmental questionnaire sought to evaluate the dynamics of regulatory convergence and how foreign companies may have influenced that process. The questionnaire was structured as follows.

General questions

This section aimed at deriving an understanding of the regulatory situation faced by the specific policy-makers.

Question 1: In what industry are you regulating companies?
Question 2: What is the basic framework for regulation? When was it developed? Who was responsible for the development of the legislation?

EU regulations and national legislation

Question 3: To what extent has national regulation been approximated and/or harmonized towards EU legislation? When, if at all, did this process start?
Question 4: What were the main issues/problems that you faced in the convergence of legislation towards EU norms?
Question 5: Do you regard EU regulations as superior to your previous national ones?

This section aims at understanding the current and future state of national regulation and the process of regulatory convergence. It is designed to gain a factual insight as well as an opinion from the regulators of their current regulatory system.

MNEs and regulation

Question 6: What influence do MNEs have on your system of regulation?
Question 7: What methods do they use to attempt to influence you?
Question 8: What degree of success do you estimate that they have had in changing the regulatory structures?

With questions 6–8, we are attempting to gather the impression of regulators' views on MNE influence on regulations and regulatory convergence. Again, we are considering both direct and indirect methods used by the companies given the open question 7.

Question 9: What role, if any, have MNEs played in raising regulatory standards in the industry by virtue of the business practices?

This is a crucial question: we are hoping to gauge the 'competitive advantage' effect of MNE activity from the perspective of the policy-maker.

Our second questionnaire, aimed at industry sources, served primarily two purposes. First, to gauge factual information from our sources on the nature of the industry, their company, and their competitors. Second to interpret the role played by foreign firms in the process of regulatory convergence. Each question is considered below.

General questions

The first section of our questionnaire considered the basic factual and strategic information about the company.

Question 1: How long have you been in Hungary?
Question 2: What were the most important factors in your decision to invest in Hungary?

With this question, we were seeking to gauge a range of strategic motives such as market potential, factor costs, regulatory environment etc.

Question 3: What is your market position/share?
Question 4: What are the short/medium/long-term strategic aims of the company in Hungary?

Here, we were seeking to analyse the FDI motives of the company. How long do they intend remaining in the industry? Is it factor costs that determine their short-term strategy? Is it long-term income growth of the market that encourages their presence?

Regulation and your business

Second, we made an attempt to assess the role played by the inter-viewee company and of their foreign competitors in the process of regulatory convergence. We looked at two main effects. First, we considered the direct role of MNEs in their attempts to change legislation. These questions were as follows:

Question 1: What are the main regulatory structures under which your company is operating?
Question 2: In what ways do Hungarian laws regulating your business resemble or replicate existing EU rules on business practices?
Question 3: If Hungarian rules differ from EU ones, what are the advantages and disadvantages of the current Hungarian framework?
Question 4: In what ways did your company influence the introduction of regulations in Hungary in the sector in which you operate?

These questions sought to gain an understanding of the company's awareness of the regulatory framework in Hungary and its similarity to that of current EU frameworks. Importantly, question 4 seeks to estimate the influence of the companies on the regulatory framework in Hungary in both a direct and indirect way.

Question 5: Do you have any formal or informal connections with public legislative/regulatory authorities?
Question 6: Is your company a member of a pressure/interest group?
Question 7: In what other ways, if any, do you participate in the legislative and regulatory process?

These questions sought to generate more specific answers to question 4 focusing explicitly on the direct and indirect influence of the companies concerned. Question 7 is especially important as it focuses on 'non-traditional' sources of influence such as those central to our study – the raising of standards through the exploitation of competitive advantage. Lastly, where sectors face greater competition from MNEs, we would expect the 'competitive advantage effect' to exert a greater influence on the speed of regulatory convergence.

Question 8: What changes do you expect in the near future (especially as a result of Hungary's accession to the EU)? What would be the main effects in your view?

Your local competitors

Question 9: Who are your local competitors?

Question 10: Which of these companies are Hungarian-owned? Foreign-owned?

Question 11: Which of your competitors do you regard as your biggest threat?

Question 12: What competitive advantage do you possess over your local rivals?

Question 13: In what way, if any, is experience of operating under EU laws a competitive advantage compared to Hungarian, local rivals?

Question 14: Have you brought EU business 'best practice' with you to Hungary?

These questions seek to engage the company in assessing the local competition and the degree to which they have been exploiting their regulatory competitive advantage over their local rivals.

As can be appreciated from these questions, we were attempting to gauge the direct political influence of the companies we interviewed; how they managed to engage in the political process in Hungary and what methods they employed to influence both administrative and legislative bodies. This is not the main thrust of our theoretical argument but it is an important issue to consider in our overall understanding of the how regulatory convergence occurs.

By combining the secondary case study material on our sectors and by using the questionnaire as the basis of our interviews we have attempted to derive our conclusions for each sector. As we are at pains to stress, the 'competitive advantage' effect is an indirect one. It can only be inferred by the statements of regulators and industry managers. However, as we shall illustrate in our cases in Chapters 6 through 8, we have been able to identify some key contributory roles played by foreign companies in the process of regulatory convergence.

We are also arguing that there is a dynamic relationship between the presence of MNEs and the introduction of EU-compliant legislation. As MNE presence intensifies in market-serving FDI, we believe there is a relationship between the intensity of MNE activity and the 'pace' with which EU-compliant regulations are introduced in the sectors that are examined.

Lastly, we would expect that where sectors face greater competition from MNEs, we would expect the 'competitive advantage effect' to exert a greater influence on the speed of regulatory convergence. Thus where MNEs face relatively little competition, the speed with which new EU-compliant legislation would be implemented would be slower than in a sector where they are required to compete with fellow MNEs or local rivals and where, consequently, they are more likely to attempt to leverage higher standards as a vehicle for competition.

5.5 Conclusion

In this chapter we have developed our empirical and conceptual methodology for exploring our case studies in the next three chapters. A central aspect of our conceptual approach has been to focus on MNEs involved in market-serving FDI since one of our principal arguments has been that in market-serving FDI, MNEs are likely to make use of higher service standards in competition with local rivals as a central vehicle of their competitive strategy.

The range of empirical material used for this study is principally from primary sources in the form of interviews with industry managers and sectoral policy-makers in government. We made use of two open-question questionnaires during our interviews that sought to engage both factual data and interpretive views on the role played by MNEs in the process of regulatory convergence. We complemented these interviews with Hungarian-language and English-language industrial reports and studies.

We would expect two effects in our case studies. First, the degree of regulatory convergence rises where the level of foreign ownership of industry rises. Thus in industries with significant MNE presence, the use of higher standards of competitive rivalry should be greater. This is linked to our second predicted effect: as the degree of competition in the sector studied rises, the necessity for the leveraging of competitive advantage effects should be higher. Thus where an MNE is granted a monopoly position in the market with little or no threat of future competition, the MNE is unlikely to be required to use higher standards. As we discuss in Chapter 9, this has significant implications for policy.

6
Banking and Financial Services

6.1 Introduction

Our first case study examines the banking and financial services sector in Hungary. Far and away the most internationalized of the ECE banking sectors, it has been subject to EU-conforming rules since 1998. As our case illustrates, it was the decision of the Hungarian state to sell the banks to strategic foreign investors that largely contributed to the speed with which Hungary could adopt EU rules into national law. Foreign banks, in largely serving MNEs based in Hungary, forced the domestic banking sector to upgrade its service provision and internal capital structures if they wished to capture a portion of the lucrative MNE market for financial services. This had a knock-on effect, forcing OTP Bank, Hungary's largest retail bank, to follow suit in the personal and small business sector if it wished to maintain its market position as the leading retail bank in Hungary. The chapter is organized as follows. Part one gives a narrative on the development of the Hungarian banking sector. Part two examines the role of FDI in the banking sector. It details the history of FDI in this sector and the changing ownership structures of the sector. Part three evaluates the role played by foreign banks in legislative approximation towards EU standards. Part four is a concluding section.

6.2 Private-sector banking in Hungary since 1989

Hungary's banking system has gone through a remarkable transformation in recent years, from being a money-losing state-owned drain on public resources in the 1980s to becoming 75 per cent privately owned and a generally sophisticated financial sector operating at Western European standards by the late 1990s. The key to this transformation has been foreign investment, to the point where up to two-thirds of Hungary's banks are now fully or partially foreign-owned. Postabank, the second largest domestic account holding bank in Hungary is to be taken over by OTP as part of a government-driven policy to solve the financial difficulties of the bank.[1]

Until the end of the communist period in Hungary in late 1989, the political authorities in the country sought to promote limited reforms without threatening the system itself. The reforms that were introduced turned out to provide a solid foundation for the completion of Hungary's transforming to a market economy in the 1990s (Estrin, Hare and Suranyi 1992). By 1982, the country had become heavily indebted (the foreign debt surpassed $10 billion that year) and was experiencing a deteriorating current account, in part due to efforts to cushion the economy from adverse international events and the growing inability of the Soviet Union to continue financing their socialist neighbours. This motivated the government to seek membership in the IMF and World Bank. About the same time, a law was passed allowing Hungarian enterprises to issue domestic bonds, which resulted in a growing bond market funded in large part by domestic savings.

In 1987, during this period of broad liberalization and the approaching end of state socialism, the Hungarian government created a two-tier banking system, separating the central bank from commercial and retail banking. Three commercial banks were created oriented towards different sectors of the economy. The principal goal of this reform was to promote competition between banks and create an effective commercial banking sector able to deal with companies without government intervention (Suranyi 1998). In 1991, another part package of banking reforms was instituted, requiring banks to:

(a) accumulate loan loss provisions and meet capital adequacy ratios of 8 per cent (the Banking Act LXIX of 1991),
(b) maintain conformity with international accounting standards (the Act on Accounting XVIII of 1991), and
(c) follow strict rules of bankruptcy and receivership (the Bankruptcy Act IL of 1991).

Unfortunately, the newly created commercial banks were left with what would become a large amount of substandard or qualified debt (according to Bank of International Settlements definitions) inherited from the previous system. At the outset of two-tiered banking, without the infrastructure in place to measure debt quality, there was little in the way of bad debt. However, after 1991, with the implementation of international credit standards, accompanied by the effects of increased market discipline on both banks and their borrowers plus a severe post-communist economic recession, qualified debt began to soar until it reached nearly 30 per cent of all debt in 1993 (Abel et al. 1998).

The continuation of state ownership after 1989 resulted in inadequate corporate governance and a lack of transparent criteria for lending, which made the outflow of credits to low-quality debtors a regular practice (Török 2000). At the same time, reforms previously enacted by the government were not rigidly enforced, and debt relief was provided to the commercial banks unconditionally which did little to enforce discipline among bank management. Under the terms of two workout programmes in 1991–2, the government took over about $1 billion, or 90 per cent of the banks' non-performing debt, with little demand for significant improvement of bank practices in return. This lack of control helped create the dismal situation where 45 per cent of loans on the books of Hungarian banks at year-end 1993 and originating in the year 1990 were classified as 'bad' (Abel et al. 1998). Fortunately, once the bank privatization process was initiated in 1994 and the government began to stipulate that banks receiving state funds should modernize their systems of internal control, the percentage of non-performing debt began to fall sharply, descending to 4 per cent of the total portfolio in 1997 (Economist 1998).

By late 1995, the government had forced the merger or liquidation of small and unprofitable banks, and began to sell the larger banks as well. To make the banks possible to sell, the government had to inject about 9 per cent of GDP into the banking system, recapitalizing banks to meet BIS standards. In troubled banks, loans were separated so that a core bank with a solid portfolio could be readied for privatization. By 1998, state ownership had descended from 67 to 20 per cent in the sector. Furthermore, this privatization was accomplished in significant part through foreign direct investment, and was undertaken

Table 6.1   Foreign and domestic shareholdings within the Hungarian banking sector

Bank	Principal shareholder	Holding %
ABN-AMRO Bank	AMN Amro Bank NV	99.85
Bank Austria Creditanstalt	BACA Int. AG	99
	Banca Intesa spa	10
Budapest Bank	Credit & Development SPHC	23.8
	Other Hungarian shareholders	12.8
	EBRD	33.6
	GE Capital	28.4
Citibank Rt	Citibank Overseas Inv Corp	100
Central European Intl Bank (CIB)	Banca Commerciale Italiana	100
Erste Bank Hungary	Erste bank Sparkassen	98.6
General Banking &	Gazprombank	42.5
Trust Co Ltd	Acma Inv. PTE	10
	Citycom Holdings	10
	Hungarian shareholders	37.5
Hungarian Foreign Trade Bank	Bank Bayerische Bank Landesbank	83.3
	Bank fur Arbeit & Wirtschaft	10.4
Eximbank	Hungarian State	100
Hypovereinsbank	Bayerische Hype und Vereinsbank	100
ING Bank (Hungary)	ING Bank NV	100
Kereskedelmi &	KBC Bank	73.3
Hitelbak (K&H)	Irish Life Plc	17.9
Raiffeisen Bank	Raiffeisen Bank Austria	95.9
Volksbank Hungary	Oesterrechishe Volksbank	61.73
Wesdeutsche Landesbank	Westdeutsche Landesbank	99.8

Source: Hungarian Banking Association.

with relative speed. Table 6.1 demonstrates the broad ownership of the Hungarian banking sector. A number of foreign banks have entered the market as Greenfield investments such as Citibank, ABN-AMRO, ING and Banca Commerciale Italia. Others have entered as joint ventures with Hungarian or other foreign partners.

Tables 6.2 and 6.3 demonstrate the profit and branch structure of the Hungarian banking sector. Two key points emerge from this data. First, OTP dominates the Hungarian sector in terms of revenue and branch numbers. The former state savings bank, it has been

Table 6.2 Top Hungarian banks (million HUF)

Rank		Bank	Balance sheet total	Profit after tax
1999	1998			
1	1	OTP Bank	1 872 383	29 643
2	2	MKB	677 845	6036
3	6	CIB	558 751	7765
4	3	K&H	546 473	−7602
5	5	ABN Amro Bank	430 780	−17 686
6	4	Postabank	346 132	−2158
7	8	Budapest Bank	307 628	1667
8	9	Bank-Austria Creditanstalt	290 600	3961
9	10	Raiffeisen Bank	259 969	4431
10	11	ÁÉB	224 308	5783
11	–	Citibank	213 759	3224
12	7	MFB	179 138	2264

Source: Figyelö Top 200.

Table 6.3 Branch numbers by bank in Hungary

Bank	Number of branches
OTP Bank	440
K&H	117
ABN-AMRO	103
Budapest Bank	75
Postabank	60
Erste Bank	55
CIB	37
Konzumbank	34
Raiffeisen	33
MKB	30
Bank Austria-Creditanstalt	25
Hypovereinsbank	19
Inter-Europa Bank	19
Citibank	17

Source: Hungarian Banking Association.

privatized through share issuance. Its management remains Hungarian. Second, there is a significant degree of foreign activity that ranges from relatively low-level services to foreign companies based in Hungary to more ambitious banking services to a broader market.[2]

6.3 FDI in the banking sector

Liberalization of the capital account of the balance of payments involves allowing both capital imports and exports, abolition of foreign exchange controls and restrictions on the activities of foreign and domestic banks, as well as allowing citizens to borrow and invest abroad (Buch 1997). Many economists believe that liberalization of the capital account should follow deregulation of the domestic financial system, and that opening domestic markets to foreign competition should be a gradual process. This would allow the protected domestic sector time to become more competitive, and avoid situations where strong foreign institutions enter a market suddenly and provide their own nationals favoured treatment to the detriment of host-country residents (Edwards and van Wijnbergen 1987).

While the theory may suggest a gradualist approach to banking and financial reform, Hungary did not follow this path, and opened the gates to foreign investment in the financial sector at an early stage of overall bank privatization. Around 44 per cent of Hungarian bank assets were owned by foreign financial institutions by 1996 (The Economist 1998). This was a greater percentage than the neighbouring countries of Poland (13.6 per cent), Czech Republic (12.6 per cent) and Slovakia (12.7 per cent), where the policies regarding foreign ownership of the financial sector were more restrictive, particularly regarding the direct market entry of foreign banks. Five years after the full-scale privatization effort began, the IMF reported that the portion of the Hungarian banking system in foreign hands exceeded 67 per cent in 2000 (Moody's 2001). In part, this was due to the lack of accumulated domestic capital in a relatively small and struggling post-communist society.[3]

In Hungary, if the banks were going to be sold by the government, foreigners would have to participate in the purchase. The Hungarian experience was also different from that of neighbouring Czech Republic and Slovakia, where instead of rapid foreign investment, privatization was through a voucher system and mutual-type investment funds, mostly run by the very banks in which they invested. This tended to create a conflict of interest which in the Czech case would lead to problems of systemic bad debt in the banking sector.

Foreign ownership has advantages, including the fact that foreign banks have easier access to capital and financial expertise in international capital markets. Outside ownership can bring sources of capital from abroad to cash-starved business in a less developed economy and can smooth out regional variations in wealth and financial opportunity.[4] The levelling effect of capital investment can be expected (absent other mitigating factors) to reduce the difference between relatively poor and wealthy regions, especially important in a country such as Hungary which desires to enjoy the living standards of EU member states.

In the literature, the process of financial reform and liberalization has been much discussed in the context of both developing countries and transforming economies. The principal difference between these two groups (for example, Mexico versus Hungary) rests in the fact that liberalization in transforming economies involves the replacement of a state-owned mono-bank with a two-tiered banking system that separates the central bank from retail/ commercial banking. Liberalization also includes the lifting of administrative controls on the activities of the commercial banks, such as the loosening of interest rate and credit controls as well as the demise of subsidized lending programmes (Buch 1997).

Domestic banks in transforming countries suffer many disadvantages, often including troublesome operational inefficiencies and low-quality assets. They often lack experienced personnel and reliable sources of information on the performance of potential borrowers, and in many cases they have inherited low quality loans from past years. The question remains: is the development of an efficient and responsive banking system which promotes economic growth in a society best obtained through rapid external liberalization, in other words, opening the market to foreign competitors?

The Hungarian experience would suggest that foreign investment in the banking sector of a transforming economy does indeed promote these goals, at least in part. The bad loans problem has improved, bank services are much better and most banks (especially the foreign-owned ones) are reasonably profitable and adequately capitalized. Recent data from Moody's (2001) has graded three major foreign-owned Hungarian banks (ABN-Amro, K&H Bank and MKB) with a very positive A3 credit rating.[5] For comparison, two domestically owned banks with large shares of household deposits received ratings of D+ (OTP Bank) and E (Postabank).

6.4 Dilemmas despite the arrival of foreign banks

However, the entry of foreign capital is no panacea to the problems of transforming economies, as disturbing gaps remain and have even grown after privatization of financial services, which foreign banks do not seem to have addressed. Two particular problems stand out. First, banks continue to lend a significant amount to the government at the expense of the private sector. Second, this diminished amount that the private sector receives in loans (after deducting public sector financing) from foreign-owned banks is not sufficiently channelled to households, which in turn limits the consumption and future capital growth of families and individuals, the foundations of the society. This strategy of foreign banks leads to two effects.

First, the presence of foreign ownership has not resolved the fact that banks are investing in government securities rather than investing in company equity. The Budapest Stock Exchange has failed to operate as expected with an absence of growth in the exchange index. While part of the problems facing the stock market in Hungary has been general instability in the region, there seem to be specific problems in Hungary that are holding back its growth. Most evident among these has been the remarkable growth of investment in commercial and residential real estate rather than in equity. Research has also shown that, generally, domestic banks in Hungary tend to hold more cash and long-term securities than foreign banks. This is due in part to the fact that domestic banks received consolidation bonds to compensate them for their bad debt, but the same overall difference between foreign and domestic banks has been noted in Poland also (Buch 1997).

Foreign bank lending has not resolved the problem of insufficient availability of private sector bank credit in Hungary, however. Table 6.4 shows the proportion of total bank assets (both foreign and domestically owned banks) representing credits to the central government in both Hungary and Poland, and one can see that the banks in Hungary still devote almost half their assets to lending to the public sector. In the banking systems of developed countries, whose ranks Hungary aspires to join, the proportion of bank assets in government securities is more similar to the figures from Poland. This data reveals that Hungarian banks, both foreign and domestic, are still quite timid in their willingness to lend to the private sector.

Table 6.4 Credits to the central government – percentage of total bank assets

Year	Hungary (%)	Poland (%)
1991	35	29
1992	38	5
1993	42	3
1994	40	1
1995	34	2
1996	41	2

Source: Abel et al. (1998) and data from the National Bank of Hungary and National Bank of Poland.

Secondly, foreign banks have shown relatively little interest in the market segments where they are most needed, which is to say retail banking, household credit, mortgage lending and small business lending, for example. Instead they tend to 'skim the cream' through dealings with only the most profitable sectors such as MNE accounts which demand a Western standard of services. As noted by Abel et al. (1998: 110), 'domestic banks and financial institutions are very inexperienced and ill-equipped to provide certain services and make markets for sophisticated products (such as options or commercial paper). They also lack the necessary infrastructure to meet Western standards in very traditional banking services for foreign and joint venture firms.' These problems are reinforced by an absence of an 'investment culture'.[6]

These sophisticated corporate segments do not require a large network of bank branches throughout the country, so the foreign banks can keep overhead costs relatively low and resulting profit margins high, which is a rational strategy for foreign banks to pursue.

However, while a corporate banking service is very important to the development of a transforming economy, the expertise of foreign banks in household consumer and mortgage lending is sorely needed to raise the standard of living in Hungary. Here the presence of foreign investment has much room for growth. This is demonstrated by the fact that the largest retail, consumer-oriented bank in Hungary is OTP Bank, which held 52.4 per cent of household deposits and 55.7 per cent of household loans in 1999 (see Table 6.5). OTP bank still has the majority of household deposits and loans.

Table 6.5   Percentage of total household deposits (and
household loans) held by individual Hungarian banks

Banks	1990	1999
MHB-ABN Amro*	1.6 (0.0)	5.4 (0.9)
K and H*	1.0 (0.2)	7.1 (2.9)
MKB*	0.9 (0.0)	10.2 (1.1)
Budapest Bank*	0.1 (0.0)	5.1 (3.9)
Postabank	2.5 (0.8)	4.3 (1.8)
OTP	93.2 (98.4)	52.4 (55.7)

*Foreign majority ownership.

A fundamental dilemma facing foreign banks in Hungary is the
need to develop a critical mass if they are to serve a mass retail market profitably. In the mid-1990s, ING Bank's entry strategy was to
challenge OTP's dominance through large-scale entry. However, less
than five years later, they had to reverse that strategic decision. The
costs of such entry were too high and customer loyalty to OTP made
it difficult to break down.[7] One of OTP's strengths is related to a
decision taken by the Hungarian state to require all state employees
to be paid directly into a bank account. For these purposes,
the Hungarian state suggested that employees open an account with
OTP. This automatically granted OTP an advantage over its foreign
rivals.

The future of the Hungarian economy rests arguably on its ability
to remain competitive *vis-à-vis* its lower cost neighbours. Hungary has
a higher GDP per capita and income level than all of its neighbours
to the north, south and east[8] so it cannot rely on cheap labour costs
alone to attract additional foreign investment. Many of its neighbours also have labour forces equally as well trained as Hungary's –
no doubt one of the few benefits of the region's communist period is
a well-educated population. Hungary does have a better infrastructure, less corruption and a more transparent legal system than most
of its post-communist neighbours, but the risk of losing this competitive advantage remains as neighbouring countries advance. One of
the most significant needs in Hungary these days is to match the
labour force supply to demand. Already, skilled labour shortages are
being noticed in the more industrialized and relatively prosperous

west and Budapest regions. On the other hand, the relatively poor east and south of Hungary suffer from both unemployment and under-employment of people, who could possibly alleviate the skills shortages in the west.

However, the housing market in Hungary remains very under-developed, and a low-income individual willing to move from some small town in the east to Györ or Székesfehervár in the booming northwest will face a very daunting task of locating affordable housing, either rental or to buy. This is where the need comes for stronger consumer banking with affordable mortgage plans and other forms of consumer loans. Foreign banks have the experience with credit reporting systems, secondary mortgage markets and all the other aspects of modern mortgage lending that could surely benefit this country if foreign bank investment were channelled in this direction.

The domestic banks and traditional savings banks (such as OTP) have access to a branch network that eases the accumulation of household savings (Buch 1997). However, foreign banks have superior assessment skills and are often better positioned to participate in the market for loans. And the creation of a sound mortgage financing system for households is one of the most significant needs of Hungary if it is to approach Western European living standards in the future. Certainly, this lack of ability to easily convert property to cash, or easily acquire capital gains producing assets is a glaring weakness throughout the developing and transforming economies, from Central and Eastern Europe to Latin America. Hungary now has strong protection of property rights incorporated into its legal system (US Department of Commerce 1999), so a key reason for lack of foreign investment in mortgage financing does not exist. The question of whether this business can be profitable for foreign-owned banks is an issue that will have to be resolved in the future.[9]

Managers in Hungary seem to be of the view that there is a 'chicken and egg' scenario here. They argue that the absence of a functioning mortgage market is due in part to a lack of consumer awareness of this kind of lending and a conservative culture among banking customers to eschew large loans.[10] Moreover, income levels in Hungary have not reached sufficiently high levels to allow consumers to borrow large enough amounts of money against their incomes.

6.5 Legislative change and foreign banks

The aim of this section is to review the various legislative changes in the Hungarian banking sector that have brought Hungarian financial legislation in conformity with current EU legislation. One of the remarkable successes of the Hungarian banking reform has been the speed with which EU legislation has been implemented. While Portugal and Spain were granted ten-year transition periods for the implementation of the free movement of capital directive, Hungary implemented full capital mobility and convertibility of the forint in July 2001 ahead of membership.

The Hungarian banking and financial services sector is governed by the Ministry of Finance, the National Bank of Hungary and the Financial Regulatory Authority. The division of labour between them is complex. However, broadly speaking, the Ministry of Finance has overall political control of financial sector regulation and delegates a series of tasks to the Financial Regulatory Authority. It is the Ministry of Finance which presents legislative proposals to the Hungarian Parliament. The Financial Regulatory Authority helps the Ministry in developing proposals in this context. The National Bank of Hungary is responsible for monetary policy and is independent of the government. It can impact on financial services regulation to the extent that it attempts to influence the monetary base in Hungary.

Hungary had already implemented a range of EU-compliant and Basle Committee-compliant legislation by the end of the 1990s. As noted in section 6.1, one of the immediate actions taken by the Hungarian state was to raise capital adequacy standards to the minimum 8 per cent (which is compliant with EU capital adequacy rules).

6.6 MNE bank strategy and regulatory convergence

In previous sections, we have debated at some length the advantages and disadvantages for a transition political economy of having substantial foreign ownership of the banking sector. We have demonstrated that while in theoretical and conceptual terms there are significant benefits, in practice, while some of the developmental benefits of foreign banks such as access to global capital markets and expertise may indeed be important, we have also seen that bank strategies to serve predominantly their fellow MNEs while based in

Hungary may have led to an undersupply of financial services and capital to individuals especially in the personal lending and mortgage sectors.

In this section, we aim to broaden our analysis to examine the link between MNE bank strategy and regulatory convergence. Throughout the interviews with managers and policy-makers linked to the Hungarian banking sector, one of the most frequently cited benefits of having foreign banks present in Hungary has been the remarkable transformation in banking practices and systems that have pushed the sector from being inefficient, high cost and using rudimentary and low technologies to being an efficient, low cost and technology-driven sector. Indeed, such is the success of the transformation of the banking sector that one senior manager suggested to us that the Hungarian sector is somewhat 'boring'.[11]

Thus in what ways has the MNE bank in Hungary aided legislative approximation? Once again, as conventional political science theories would suggest, the foreign banks have been active in pursuing a lobbying agenda with the Hungarian state to introduce EU-compliant legislation.[12] This direct form of political influence is clear and conforms comfortably to our understanding of political action of MNEs.

However, we are interested more in the relationship between competitive advantage as a business strategy and the introduction of EU-conforming legislation. The large-scale arrival of foreign banks in the mid-1990s soon led the general framework for banking in Hungary to be in conformity with the EU Second Banking Directive as early as 1 January 1997.[13] The Second Banking Directive is a far-reaching legal instrument based on the concept of mutual recognition, which has been the cornerstone of the Single Market project in the EU. Prior to the introduction of the Second Banking Directive in 1989, regulation of foreign banks was governed by the host-country principle. This meant that the local financial regulators had the right to impose specific controls on foreign banks that may not need to be applicable to domestic banks and financial entities. This, arguably, had the effect of discriminating against foreign banks and restricting competition in domestic markets.[14] In any case, the host-country principle created an additional non-tariff barrier (NTB) that needed to be removed if the completion of Single Market as envisaged by EU legislators was to be achieved.

The Second Banking Directive shifted banking supervision from the host-country to the home-country principle thereby eliminating this NTB and creating a 'Single Banking Licence' for banks operating in the EU. This important regulatory change implied that if foreign banks were regulated at home, that would be sufficient for them to operate anywhere in the EU.[15] This was a far-reaching outcome that led to considerable cross-border mergers and acquisitions of financial services providers in the EU.[16] It created a 'level playing field' for all EU-licensed credit institutions which enabled banks to adopt a European, rather than a domestic, strategy in their banking practices.

The Hungarian delegation involved in negotiating Hungarian accession to the EU was able to close the Financial Services chapter of the negotiations among the first ten they completed.[17] In July 2001, the Hungarian state implemented the Capital Movements Directive which allows for the elimination of all capital controls in Hungary and complete convertibility of the forint.

Another important milestone achieved by Hungarian financial regulation has been the achievement of capital adequacy ratios for credit institutions of above the EU mandated 8 per cent. Indeed current mean capital adequacy ratios are of the order of 14 per cent.[18] Capital adequacy is an important test of a bank's solvency and its ability to make prudent operations given the amount of reserves it has to cover its possible losses.

This is a remarkable achievement in less than a decade. At the time of writing, Hungary was the first among the current candidate countries to have introduced the Second Banking Directive in such a far-reaching way. We argue that this is directly related to the role played by foreign banks in the introduction of the EU legislation.

Problems still exist, however. Notably, while the EU-conforming Hungarian banking law allows for the establishment of branches of foreign firms, the high level of bureaucratic regulation has effectively qualified foreign bank branches as subsidiaries rather than branches. However, the Hungarian negotiators have committed to repealing these provisions upon accession to the EU. In a similar vein, Hungarian deposit insurance levels are below those recommended by EU standards. Since, in closing the Financial Services chapter of the negotiations, the Hungarian state did not request derogation on deposit insurance, it has committed itself to introducing the necessary legislation upon accession.[19]

So what part of foreign bank strategy has contributed to the introduction of EU legislation in Hungary? On the basis of our interviews, one facet of the MNE bank strategy has emerged as important in this context: the creation of professionalism and awareness of an investment culture among senior bankers in Hungary. Foreign banks have significantly impacted on business practices in that the introduction of foreign bankers into the sector and the training of younger, new managers have been central to upgrading service standards in the sector.

Second, the role of technology and payments systems brought by foreign banks has aided the development of a modern banking infrastructure in Hungary such as the creation of an efficient network of automatic teller machines (ATM) and other automatic payments systems.

Third, central to the foreign bank's overall market strategy has been to claim to prospective clients (predominantly foreign firms and new Hungarian companies) that they have market expertise and know-how that the local competitors simply do not have. This has had both direct and indirect effects. In terms of direct effects, probably the most important has been that foreign banks have been able to capture substantial business among the foreign companies present in Hungary. This had led to an indirect effect that has forced domestic rivals either to improve their service or face losing clients. This exploitation of competitive advantage, as we have noted in our research, has led to an improvement in the overall level of service provided in the sector and, consequently, the adjustment costs that implementing EU conforming legislation would have, have been substantially lower as competition between local and foreign banks on the basis of higher commercial standards has already set the adjustment process in train. This implies that there was less political resistance to the implementation of EU legislation in Hungary because local companies, who we would expect to resist higher standards given the costs involved in upgrading their service standards, were already close to or operating at the EU level standards.

This is a compelling result that suggests that, on a broader level, market-serving FDI-induced competition, rather than leading to a regulatory spiral downwards as companies compete to offer ever lower standards as a means of competition (through lowering price), actually leads to an improvement in industry standards and a regulatory spiral upwards.[20]

6.7 Conclusions

This chapter has examined in depth the development of the Hungarian banking sector and the role played by foreign banks in general and more specifically in relation to the process of convergence with and implementation of EU legislation in the Hungarian sector.

One of the most tangible benefits of the presence of foreign companies has been the overall improvement in banking infrastructure, service provision and technological upgrading that these entities have brought with them. Moreover, their access to foreign capital markets has brought much-needed capital restructuring in the period after 1989 especially in the reform of bad debt and loans. While as we have noted, foreign banks have been largely serving foreign companies based in Hungary, the emergence of K&H bank and ABN-AMRO bank as potential competitors for OTP bank suggests that on a retail level, we may also experience a significant improvement in choice available to customers. As yet, personal lending and mortgage markets remain somewhat underdeveloped owing to a combination of unattractive cost requirements to supply these services on the part of foreign banks and the low level of personal income and conservative attitudes of Hungarian customers.

Of more direct interest to our research has been the link between foreign bank strategy and the implementation of EU-compliant legislation. As we have noted above, Hungary is one of the first of the candidate countries to have closed the Financial Services chapter in the accession negotiations. On a range of regulatory issues, current Hungarian laws set standards equivalent to EU levels and the actual performance of the sector in the case of capital adequacy actually exceeds those levels themselves. While other candidate countries have yet to implement a legal framework for financial services close to EU standards, the Hungarian state had already implemented the Second Banking Directive and most of its related provisions by 1998. We believe that the success of Hungarian regulatory convergence is a direct consequence of foreign banks leveraging their competitive advantage to create a higher standard, lower cost and more competitive banking sector. The adjustment costs associated with legislative changes as envisaged by EU accession for Hungary have already been somewhat mitigated by the presence of foreign banks, which are already operating at EU standards and, through the competitive game, have forced local rivals to raise their standards. Altogether, traditional pressures from local companies for maintaining the status quo have been lower as a consequence of this, thereby enabling legislators in the Hungarian Parliament to push through the new laws.

7
The Electricity Sector

7.1 Introduction

Following on from our previous case study of the banking and financial services sector, in this chapter we consider the electricity sector and the extent of regulatory convergence towards EU rules. As with the banking sector, foreign ownership of the sector has been extensive in Hungary with the Hungarian state deciding to sell companies to strategic investors from the US and West Europe (especially German companies). In fact, energy companies were some of the first companies to be sold by the Hungarian state to foreign investors. There was considerable debate as to whether the price for the companies that the foreign energy firms paid was a fair one. However, the income raised by the government contributed to paying off Hungary's significant external debt.[1]

While the introduction of EU legislation in the banking sector was related to the creation of open markets, liberalization of the electricity sector and the creation of competition were more complex than the sale of companies and the removal of restrictions on certain kinds of transactions. Indeed, as the experience in West Europe and North America has shown, privatization does not guarantee competition in the traditional sense. A period of significant market regulation is required before competition can ensue. Moreover, companies who invest in the electricity sector normally require a period of monopoly in order for them to recoup the significant investments they make in capital and infrastructure.

In the absence of a temporary monopoly, there would be few incentives to upgrade the capital and infrastructure in the sector.[2] By the same token, through forms of price controls and service mandates regulators ensure that the monopolists do not overcharge consumers and maintain a reasonable level of service standards. This trade-off is a difficult and challenging issue for regulators – Hungary being no exception in this case. One of the important aspects to remember is that in a transition political economy such as Hungary, there is limited need for new investment in new capacity due to a fall in demand for electricity as a consequence of the economic transition process. It is also unlikely that demand for electricity is likely to rise above pre-1989 levels and thus investment in capacity is mainly for upgrading of capital to meet environmental pressures and also to link the sector to the West European network. Thus regulation of the sector is unlikely to be driven by the need for new capacity creation.

Pressures on the Hungarian state to meet the terms of EU liberalization directives have added additional issues for the regulators. In the absence of EU accession considerations, it may have been the case that the Hungarian authorities would have allowed for monopolies to last longer.

The main findings from our research are that unlike the banking sector, where foreign banks have leveraged their competitive advantage in a competitive game with local companies, the role of foreign ownership in the electricity sector has been useful predominantly through the substantial upgrading of the infrastructure and capital in the sector. Moreover, Western management techniques have aided the privatized companies in their management systems and in dealing with customers. In a similar way to the banking sector, however, the presence of these positive effects on the sector has reduced the potential adjustment costs faced by the industry in the face of liberalization. This has reduced political resistance to liberalization along EU guidelines and hence enabled the Hungarian state to close the electricity section of the energy chapter without the need for transition periods. Once again, the presence of foreign companies has aided the process of regulatory convergence.

The chapter is organized as follows. Part one is a detailed analysis of the Hungarian electricity sector. It discusses ownership structures and the development of the sector. Part two deals with legislative and regulatory issues in the Hungarian electricity sector. Part three attempts to draw a link between foreign ownership and regulatory convergence. Part four is a concluding section.

7.2 Development of the electricity sector

As with the banking sector, the Hungarian government sought rapid liberalization of the electricity sector after 1989. The basic competitive model was based on the UK approach to liberalization of utilities[3] by creating competition among suppliers and distributors alike. The first pilot privatization was the main Csepel electricity plant which was sold to the UK electricity generator Powergen. This was undertaken as a precursor to the main privatization process. According to those involved in the privatization process, Hungarian authorities learned a lot from the pilot process that made the main privatization generally professional and well organized.[4]

It is important to emphasize at the start that Hungary was among the few Central European countries that had a fully private-owned energy sector before 1945. Figure 7.1 illustrates the different sources of electricity generation. On the generation side of the electricity sector, most of Hungary's electricity is generated by hydrocarbon and coal-based power plants. The Hungarian state still maintains

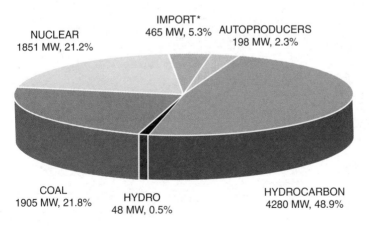

IMPORT*
465 MW, 5.3%

AUTOPRODUCERS
198 MW, 2.3%

NUCLEAR
1851 MW, 21.2%

COAL
1905 MW, 21.8%

HYDRO
48 MW, 0.5%

HYDROCARBON
4280 MW, 48.9%

Figure 7.1 Source-side capacity of the Hungarian power system (December 2000) (*Source*: MvM Rt)

a state-owned nuclear power plant supplying a substantial amount of Hungary's peak energy needs.

Hungary has electricity high-voltage transmission lines of 750 kilovolts (kV), 400 kV and 220 kV; these measure approximately 270, 1730 and 1200 kilometres in overall length, respectively. There is also a 120 kV grid which is directly supplied by many of Hungary's power plants, including the Paks nuclear power plant. The main power transmission line linking Hungary to the east is a 750 kV line from Ukraine. Hungary's higher voltage electricity transmission grid is shown in Figure 7.2.

In recent years, the Hungarian power system has become integrated into the power system of Western Europe. The connection of the Hungarian system to the West European UCPTE system was completed in 1995. A 400 kV interconnection was put into operation between Hungary and Croatia in November 1999.

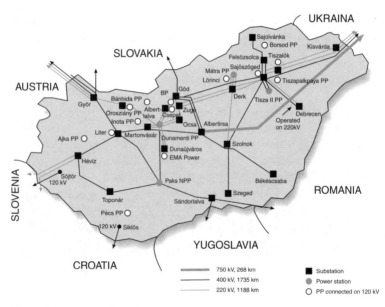

Figure 7.2 Hungary's high-voltage electricity transmission system (*Source*: MVM)

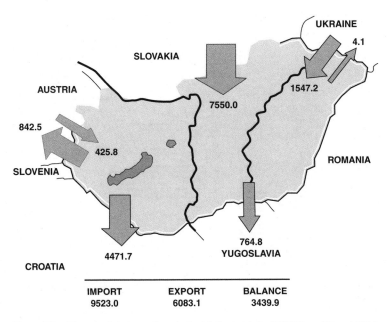

Figure 7.3   Hungary's international electricity trade in 2000 (in million kWh)

There has been a dramatic reorientation of Hungarian electricity import supply in the last decade. In 1990, Hungary had imported 12.2 billion kWh per year from Ukraine. However, by 2000, the net imports from Ukraine had shrunk to 1.54 billion kWh per year, as Hungary integrated its electric transmission with its Western neighbours. In 2000, Slovakia was Hungary's main source of imported electric power with 7.55 billion kWh per year in electricity purchases. A diagram of Hungary's international electricity trade for the year 2000 is shown in Figure 7.3.

The industry was organized along regional distribution lines with generators being located primarily on the basis of the kind of materials used to generate energy. As can be readily noted from the data in Figure 7.4, the Hungarian electricity sector has substantial foreign ownership both in terms of generation and distribution of energy.

When the generating companies were privatized in the early 1990s, the power plants were privatized in package deals with their associated coal mines. The Matra Power Company encompassed the Visonta

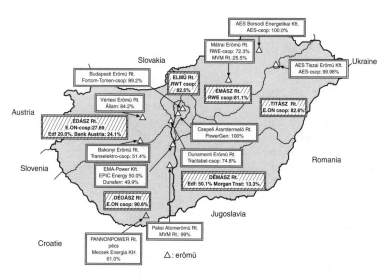

Figure 7.4   Ownership of electricity generators and suppliers (*Source*: Hungarian Energy Office)

and Bukkabrany lignite surface mines. The Bakony Power Company included the Padrag, Armin, Jokai and Balinka coal mines. The Pecs Power Company got the Kulfejtes and Komlo mines. The Vertes Power Company got the Oroszlany and Many mines. As originally structured, the Tisza Power Company included the Borsod, Tisza-palkonya, and Tisza 2 power plants, the Borsod coal plant, and the Lyukobanya mine. Later it was decided that the Borsod and Tisza-palkonya power plants would be separately privatized as Borsod Energetic Limited. Transfers of coal properties to power companies were accomplished by giving a one-quarter share to SZESZEK, the Hungarian Coal Mining Restructuring Company.

The largest foreign companies involved in the Hungarian sector are EdF (Electricité de France), E.ON and RWE from Germany, Tractabel from Belgium and AES from the USA. They are involved in both power generation and distribution. Figure 7.4 breaks down ownership of the electricity industry by nationality. As can be seen, foreign companies own more than half of the industry, with German firms having the largest interest. It is worth bearing in mind that the transmitter monopoly held by the state-owned MvM Rt and the continued state ownership of nuclear power skew the data and underestimate the presence of foreign companies. In some senses, the ownership structure in the Hungarian sector mirrors similar processes in West Europe. In particular, the role of German energy companies in Hungary has been part of the privatization process in Germany. Thus for example, in 1997, EnBW was created after the merger of Badenwerk and EVS. In 2000, RWE, one of the more important German companies based in Hungary, acquired VEW, and E.ON was created in the same year by the merger of VIAG (Bayernwerk) and VEBA (Preussen Elektra).[5] The privatization and merger activity in Germany created the necessary capital in order to allow for the acquisition of foreign companies. Table 7.1 outlines ownership of the electricity by nationality.

Hungary has privatized its distribution sector on the basis of regional companies, thus granting regional supply monopolies to the distributing companies. According to industry and regulatory sources, this was in order to encourage foreign ownership. Regional monopolies

Table 7.1 Ownership of the Hungarian electricity sector by nationality, December 2000

Owners	Producers	Transmitters	Distributors	Total industry
Hungarian state	10.22	99.86	0.10	39.26
Local authorities	0.35	0.11	3.64	1.70
Hungarian investors	55.98	0.02	10.87	7.52
Total Hungarian	**66.55**	**99.99**	**14.61**	**48.49**
German	8.59	0	63.04	30.07
French	0	0	11.83	4.85
Belgian	8.70	0	0	4.30
British	1.71	0	0	0.84
US	9.54	0	2.05	5.56
Finnish	2.26	0	0	1.12
Japanese	2.18	0	0	1.08
Others	0.02	0	7.63	3.13
Total foreign participation	**33.00**	**0**	**84.55**	**50.95**
Not registered	0.45	0.01	0.84	0.56
Total	**100.00**	**100.00**	**100.00**	**100.00**

Source: Hungarian Energy Office.

granted the companies sufficient returns on their investment.[6] Prices for electricity are still on the basis of administered prices.

Until 1992, the electricity industry was managed by the Hungarian Power Company Magyar Villamos Müvek Reszvenytarsag (MVM Rt). In 1992, Hungary reorganized MVM Rt into a two-tier company structure. The upper tier, which remained MVM Rt, manages all trade in electricity. MVM Rt owns and operates the high voltage transmission grid and dispatching centre. It purchases power from electricity generating companies and sells it to smaller distribution companies. MVM Rt controls the financial flow of electricity-based goods and services by the use of tariffs. It also manages all electricity-related import and export transactions.

The second tier of the utility system, as of 1997, was composed of eight generating companies grouped regionally and according to fuel mix; six regional distribution companies; and one maintenance company for the basic network.

For 1998 electricity production, 38 per cent was nuclear, 34 per cent was natural gas and 27 per cent was coal. The remaining 1 per cent was oil or hydroelectric. There are three small hydro plants in Hungary that generate less than half of 1 per cent of the electricity. Because MVM Rt buys electricity from the generating companies at different prices that reflect generating costs, the practical effect is that low-cost nuclear power generated at the Paks power station subsidizes most other generating plants. The MVM Rt is planning a retrofit of 300–700 MWe of existing capacity and to construct new plants of 1000–1100 MWe capacity by the year 2006. This new capacity expansion was internationally tendered in 1997 by MVM Rt.

Figure 7.5 shows the volume of electricity in trillions of watt hours (TWh) sold to each of the regional companies. Industry analysts believe that distribution and generating companies are essentially similar in their strategies: they attempt to both generate and distribute electricity.[7] This allows them to exploit economies of scale and scope in the sector.

This effectively does not allow for competition among the generators to supply the distributors. The Hungarian Energy Office pushed for full liberalization of the electricity sector in line with current EU Directives on electricity liberalization.[8] According to a survey carried out by the Hungarian Energy Office in December 2000, customer satisfaction among both industrial and consumer sectors was higher

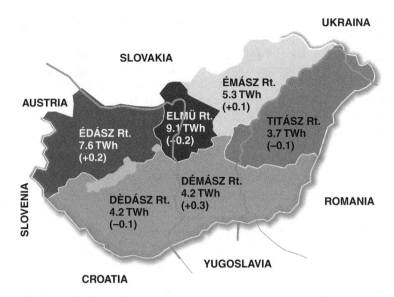

Figure 7.5 Sale of electricity by MvM Rt to regional distribution companies (*Source:* MvM Rt)

than in 1996 when the new system of regulation came into place.[9] This brings us to the fundamental question of the benefits of foreign ownership that have been brought to the Hungarian energy sector. In interviews for this research with managers and regulators, the overwhelming image is that foreign ownership motives on the part of foreign companies were not really the same as those of the privatizing agencies.[10]

The Hungarian state was hoping to sell the industry to foreigners to achieve two fundamental aims. First, they aimed to raise foreign reserves to finance Hungary's foreign debt obligations accumulated in the years before 1989 and in the early 1990s. Second, they hoped to modernize the electricity sector by bringing in foreign capital and processes. The strategic intent of the foreign companies was markedly different – especially on the distribution side. First, the considerable investment made by these companies meant that they were pushing for long-term licence agreements.[11] This was to allow them to recoup their investment – especially as they were not allowed to compete with each other to distribute electricity. Moreover, the system of administered prices to transmit electricity through MVM Rt meant that foreign companies could not seek out other sources of electricity generation. As the Hungarian state was keen to sell off the companies quickly, the distributing companies were able to secure the long-term contracts they sought. Second, as the distributing companies were effectively operating as regional monopolists, they faced no strategic threat from new entrants into their 'region'. This meant that fixed investment on the distribution side of the sector was not as high as the Hungarian state would have wished for.[12]

As the data in Table 7.1 illustrates, foreign ownership on the generation side of the electricity sector remained small (with foreign ownership making up only one-third of ownership). This can be attributed to the fact that the Hungarian state did not see such an urgent need to upgrade the generation side of the sector as it had already been well-capitalized before privatization. Moreover, the strategic implications of ownership of electricity generation meant that the Hungarian state wished to maintain control, e.g. ownership of nuclear power generation. Nevertheless, and in contrast to the distribution side of the sector, industry sources suggest that foreign ownership has enhanced quality of supply and general practices in the industry as well as helping the industry adjust to the conditions set by EU rules in the energy sector.[13]

An illustration of the financial turnaround in the sector can be grasped by data on profitability of the industry. Table 7.2 illustrates that foreign ownership of the sector has been accompanied by

Table 7.2   Operating performance of electricity companies (million HUF)

	1994	*1995*	*1996*	*1997*	*1998*	*1999*	*2000*
Subscribed capital	804,955	799,366	806,154	816,654	802,507	733,201	727,297
Own capital		867,078	795,411	768,724	790,183	803,824	849,423	854,148
Revenue		351,323	445,340	445,340	788,500	945,749	1,059,235	1,128,570
Profits before taxes		−14,737	−73,758	−42,401	18,427	54,812	85,500	73,448

Source: Hungarian Energy Office.

increasing profitability. It is likely that these profits derive from both efficiency and monopoly sources. On the efficiency side, the arrival of FDI brought more effective strategies and managerial systems to the sector. On the monopoly side, the long-term exclusive contracts negotiated by the electricity suppliers probably means that an absence of competition maintained prices in the sector. As can be seen from the data, the industry achieved reasonable revenue and profit streams by 2000. It is also worth noting that this has occurred at the same time as the companies' own capital injections have remained reasonably constant.

The majority of Hungarian energy is now imported from abroad. Domestic sources of electricity generation are made from nuclear, lignite and coal sources. Indeed, it is unlikely that a significant amount of electricity will continue to be produced domestically, suggesting that the medium to long-term survival of the electricity power plants is secure.[14]

Hungary has four pressurized-water nuclear reactors operating at Paks. Paks maintains an excellent safety record, ranked in the top 10 per cent of reactors worldwide. As a result of an extensive upgrading programme started in 1996, the power station now meets international and EU requirements for safety standards and for hazardous emissions. The authorities and management are currently investigating a long-term solution for nuclear waste disposal.[15]

7.3 Regulatory issues

In this section, we first examine general regulatory principles in the electricity sector. In Europe, the UK has led the way in the privatization and regulation of the electricity sector. While we don't claim that the regulatory framework in the UK is the 'ideal' one, it has served as an exemplar for other countries. The essential basis of the approach is to separate generation and distribution of electricity. Thus while the generation of electricity can be done by several companies on a competitive basis, the network itself has to remain largely as a monopoly regulated by a governmental authority.

In the initial phases, in the period where it is not possible to have competition for supply of electricity, the standard approach to pricing electricity for end-users was to apply an 'RPI-X' formula where RPI stands for the retail price index. This has been the standard approach taken in virtually all EU countries and also in the USA.[16] Indeed, given the natural monopoly characteristics of electricity distribution, it is unlikely that an alternative competitive distribution model could be set up. As for the generation side of the sector, given appropriate time to allow for restructuring and competition to emerge, it is feasible to have a choice of electricity suppliers for consumers. Most deregulation allowed for business customers and large users to have access to choice first, followed by more generalized liberalization for domestic customers. In this sense, the Hungarian approach has not differed substantially from the most common approach elsewhere in Europe.

There are two main future issues facing the foreign owners of electricity companies. First, the Electricity Act in Hungary has set in place the mechanisms for full liberalization of the sector in line with EU accession. New competition is likely to require a strategic reorientation for the companies who until now have been granted long-term contracts. Second, the issue of the contracts themselves is a problem for the Hungarian state and the companies. As competition has been introduced before the contracts expire, the companies may sue the Hungarian state for breach of contract. The Hungarian state is under pressure to meet the terms of EU liberalization and therefore it is likely that various compensation mechanisms will be introduced to compensate the companies.[17] RWE has asked for a 10 billion HUF compensation to be bought out of its contract. The company argued that it took on the contract on the basis that it would have sufficient time to recoup its investment as a monopolist. Competition, of course, threatens this position. Indeed, liberalization in West Europe had already negatively impacted the electricity companies' profitability.[18] When the original licences were issued, the Hungarian regulators did not anticipate EU accession as quickly as it appears to be happening.

The Hungarian state set up a committee on the energy sector consisting of government officials, industry representatives and trade unions. This group attempted to reach agreement on a common position to take to the negotiations in Brussels. After long discussions, the Hungarian negotiators were able to present a unified position.[19]

In 1999, the Hungarian delegation negotiating EU accession and chapter 14 dealing with energy made clear the intention of the Hungarian state to implement the *acquis communautaire* in this field and that it required neither derogation from the rules nor any transition periods. In the statement, the Hungarian negotiators stated:

> Hungary will proceed with the liberalization of the electricity market according to the procedures provided for by Directive 96/92/EC concerning the common rules in the internal market for electricity. This process will be gradual. Some measures are expected to be introduced as from 1 January 2001 ensuring a partial opening of the electricity market, while the whole regime in full conformity with the Directive will be effective on the date of accession.[20]

The Hungarian negotiators have already closed the energy chapter of the negotiations, once again demonstrating the relatively rapid manner in which the Hungarian state is preparing for accession.

In 2000, the EU Commission reported that Hungary had already adopted the main principles of the internal energy market and continues to implement them. The framework for further alignment with the *acquis* was set with the adoption of the long-term energy strategy in July 1999. According to the EU Commission, developments in the *acquis* must be taken into account when implementing the principles. Unresolved issues include further liberalization in preparation for the internal energy market, energy efficiency, the promotion of renewable energy sources and security of supply.

In this connection, progress continued on preparation for the internal market, with the government submitting a draft law on electricity in early 2000, which provided for a limited test opening of the market in Hungary in January 2002 (around 15 per cent of the total annual consumption). The largest industrial users will be allowed to choose their electricity suppliers. Third-party access to the grid will begin then, and independent power suppliers will be allowed to 'wheel' power through the grid, though the grid operator will be allowed to add a transport/access tariff. This competitive market is expected to eventually result in a rate decrease of as much as 15 per cent for customers. One effect of this liberalization plan is the creation of two parallel markets for electricity. The transitional public utility market will still have an official price for electricity, with the Hungarian national electricity company, MVM Rt, as the wholesaler; this will cover the 65 per cent of the market not initially affected by the first stage of market liberalization, and will gradually diminish as the competitive market expands. The public utility market should entirely disappear no later than 2010.[21]

MVM Rt has been restructured in order to facilitate EU liberalization rules implementation. It has been split into two companies: MVM Rt and MAVIR Rt. The latter will act as controller of the power system independent of MVM Rt. The idea behind this is to have a company that would offer equal access to the electricity network as MVM Rt itself produces a large amount of electricity.[22]

7.4 The role of foreign ownership and regulatory convergence

Unlike in the banking sector where regulatory convergence has been enhanced by virtue of the leveraging of competitive advantage held by foreign banks in a competitive game with local rivals, the role of foreign companies in the Hungarian electricity sector and their contribution to the process of regulatory convergence has been predominantly in preparing the industry for competition on a European scale.[23] This has been achieved in three principal ways. First, significant investment in infrastructure and finance capital has contributed to the upgrading of the industry and the efficiency of electricity generation and distribution. Investment in environmentally cleaner technologies has been significant.[24] For example, when Powergen built the new Csepel power plant, they invested over $250 million. As part of that investment, over $2 million was used for environmental clean-up of the brown field site.[25] Privatization led to significant flows of technology and capital from Austria, Germany, the US and UK as plants and infrastructure in the sector were upgraded and reconstructed.[26] As part of the reconstructed sector, new companies have been set up to service the new electricity companies.

Second, the role of West European management techniques and processes has streamlined operational tasks and systems. This has had a profound impact on the sector in a number of ways related to health and safety procedures, environmental management and human resource procedures. This has important implications for the sector in terms of the implementation of EU industrial directives. Foreign companies, Powergen, EdF and RWE have all implemented health and safety requirements that have become benchmarks for other sectors and used by Hungarian health and safety officials as examples of EU-level standards.[27] In the environmental field, the safe disposal of materials used to generate electricity, clean-up and efficient supply of electricity have met EU requirements on the environment and once again leads to a ratcheting up of standards across the sector.

Lastly, the substantial number of redundancies that have occurred as the new owners of the sector undertook a rationalization of employment required the use of high quality human resource systems that once again set a benchmark for Hungarian companies in dealing with the difficult task of employment reduction in the process of economic transition.[28] On the positive side, there has been an important transfer of skills to local employees as virtually all of the foreign companies have replaced their expatriate staff with local managers.

Third, the foreign companies that acquired the Hungarian electricity sector regarded acquisition of the Hungarian companies as part of a broader European strategy and would allow them to exploit economies of scale in the industry. In doing so, they would be able to lower industry costs and raise productive and process efficiency. Many of the foreign companies already had significant ownership in other countries and thus technical expertise, parts and systems replacements were readily available from neighbouring countries.

If we consider these contributions to the implementation of EU liberalization rules in Hungary, we can see that all three can have a positive impact. Greater competition necessarily implies that in order to remain competitive, electricity companies need to lower costs. Reinvesting in industry infrastructure, while reducing profit streams in the short run, will ensure that companies can survive cost-price based competition as a result of liberalization. The second benefit brought to the sector by foreign companies has been the introduction of West European management techniques. During the Single European Market (SEM) programme, one of the main benefits of the creation of the SEM was the reduction and or elimination of 'X-inefficiency' related to overly bureaucratic management structures. It is likely that the arrival of foreign companies in the electricity sector has been to revolutionize payments and remuneration systems, accounting processes, as well as more general managerial functions. The third benefit to the Hungarian electricity sector has been its embedding in a broader European industry as part of the foreign companies' business strategies. This allows for access to a broader range of suppliers and for the exploitation of economies of scale in a range of processes in the industry. It also allows for access to broader sources of finance for the industry.

Brought together these factors have had a profound and largely positive impact on the electricity sector and the ability of Hungarian legislators to move the sector towards EU compliance. The embedding of the necessary structural conditions for competition, through investment in the industry, has placed Hungarian electricity companies in a reasonably strong position in terms of liberalization. It has certainly reduced the pressure on legislators to slow down the introduction of EU-compliant legislation. This is the case even if the companies themselves would prefer to minimize competition. Indeed, as our research suggests, there was little or no resistance from the industry in either the negotiations with the EU member states over accession and the energy sector or in the legislative debate in the Hungarian Parliament.

With the implementation of the new Electricity Act, it is likely that competition will lead to consolidation in the sector. This is along the lines of similar consolidations across other European electricity industries. Cost efficiency is the key to survival in the sector and this could be achieved by consolidation. It will be interesting to note how the Hungarian competition authorities will deal with this process.

7.5 Conclusions

Our second case study has further developed our conceptual claim relating FDI and regulatory convergence. Rather than placing the relative success of regulatory convergence in the Hungarian electricity sector at the foot of competitive advantage used by foreign companies based around the provision of higher service standards, the narrative that has emerged in the electricity sector has been the ability of foreign companies to embed their Hungarian strategy in a broader European strategy through improvements in managerial processes; increased investment in the sector – especially in environmentally sound technologies and in exploiting network economies of scale and scope related to the relationship between generation and distribution of energy.

These three factors have led to the development of an industry that is ready to face liberalization upon accession to the EU. In some senses, West European and North American electricity companies have also played an important learning role for the industry. As pointed out in interviews for our research, the foreign companies had to face competition and liberalization in their domestic industries and so while not wholeheartedly in favour of competition because of the impact on profitability, they nevertheless were able to bring expertise of a liberalized environment to the Hungarian sector. In contrast to narratives of liberalization attempts in current EU member states, where domestic producers and suppliers have attempted to resist energy sector liberalization, there has been a distinct lack of political resistance in Hungary. It is ironic that the Hungarian electricity sector will be probably more liberalized than some current EU member states but is a testament to the profound impact of the MNE in this sector.

8
Telecommunications

8.1 Introduction

Our third case study looks at another key industry for the development of a transition political economy. Telecommunications are arguably one of the key infrastructures of the future alongside energy and finance. In terms of our FDI classification, telecommunications services are also a market-serving form of FDI. We would expect therefore that MNE strategy in these sectors would be based on a longer-term strategy than a shorter-term resource-seeking one.

Moreover, because the essence of telecommunications services is the rapid, seamless supply of differing forms of data, MNEs seeking to gain a competitive advantage would aim to use higher service standards as a tool of competitive rivalry. In the context of Hungary's accession to the EU, we seek to examine the link between the convergence of Hungary's Communications Act with EU regulations and the arrival of MNEs in the telecommunications services sector. As will become clear in the following chapter, as with both the electricity and the banking sectors, the role of MNEs in facilitating the introduction of EU-compliant legislation in Hungary has been profound and manifest. As frequently pointed out in interviews and from a range of other sources, the role of foreign companies in bringing in much needed capital and technology to the industry, in introducing EU management processes and in raising the service provision standard, has been important. This has enabled Hungary to bring the new Communications Act into force in December 2001.

However, the role of MNEs in the sector has not been completely without its problems. In particular, the decision of the Hungarian state to grant exclusive concession rights to the privatized telephone company MATÁV has enabled its majority owners Deutsche Telekom to reap significant profits from the quasi-monopoly position it has held in the market for basic, fixed-line telephony. It is arguable that MATÁV's monopoly position has held back the use of Internet services from fixed lines and made Hungarian Internet services the most expensive in the OECD.

With the coming into force of the Communications Act (2001), the exclusive rights came to an end and competition in fixed-line telephony were introduced. However, when the initial twenty-five-year concession contract was signed between MATÁV and the Hungarian state, the exclusivity of the contract was to last for eight years. Because pressures related to EU accession required the Hungarian state to introduce the new EU-compliant legislation, MATÁV was 'compensated' for ending the exclusive rights a year early. The amount of compensation was never made public nor was the actual agreement itself.[1] This was a similar experience to that of the electricity sector explored in Chapter 7 where the electricity companies were granted long-term franchise agreements which the Hungarian state has had to renegotiate because of EU energy liberalization directives.

This chapter is structured as follows. Part one provides a brief history of the development of the telecommunications services technology and regulation. Part two examines the changing ownership and market structure of the Hungarian telecommunications sector. Part three analyses the link between the new Communications Act and the role played by foreign companies in Hungary. Part four is a concluding section.

8.2 Technological convergence and telecommunications services

Unlike in the electricity sector where the market structure is relatively stable, it is a widely held view that technological convergence in the telecommunications sector is one of the most important changes occurring in industry in general today. Three industries – media, informatics and telecommunications – appear to be converging to form a new, complex value chain to provide an ever-broadening range of services to end-users. In particular, it is worth noting that the Internet and mobile telephony are providing new opportunities to transmit ever larger amounts of media content and data to end-users. The television set, which in the past was used to broadcast a limited range of terrestrial-based television programming, is likely to become a multi-tasking piece of technology allowing users to make video calls, carry out transactions on the Internet, send e-mails and watch pay-per-view digital cable television products.

In terms of the development of the technology to create these new forms of services and products, there is a tension between the need to introduce competition among potential providers of these services and the need to integrate vertically along the telecommunications value chain. It is unlikely that in the absence of competition, new technologies will emerge given the absence of incentives to do so. Moreover, an absence of choice for consumers is likely to lead to higher prices and hence under-consumption of telecommunications services. On a macroeconomic level, given the fact that telecommunications services are part of the overall economic infrastructure, this may lead to macroeconomic under-performance in terms of economic growth, employment creation and the price level.

However, both high sunk costs (and their associated risks) in R&D in telecommunications and potential economies of scale involved in vertical integration of the value chain imply the need for consolidation and co-operation in the industry to develop the new technologies themselves.

In an EU context, this dilemma has been partly reconciled by the notion of creating an EU-wide liberalized market for telecommunications services. The principal argument is that, at a national level, markets are too small to allow for several competitors and the achievement of minimum efficient scale at the same time. By liberalizing the EU market by breaking down national market segmentation, both a pluralistic supply and the achievement of scale economies for several competitors can take place by the provision of cross-border telecommunications services.

The implication for small transition political economies is that they should liberalize their telecommunications services sector in order to 'embed' the market in a larger, transnational market.

At the same time, governments and regulators are of course sensitive to the demands for protection from national telecommunications service providers who fear the increasing competition that liberalization of the market would imply. Thus, with notable exceptions such as the UK, liberalization has been a gradualist process as regulators have attempted to reconcile the need to facilitate technological process through technological convergence and the demands for protection from national suppliers. It is worth noting that of the three sectors involved in telecommunications convergence, different degrees of liberalization have taken place. Of the three sectors, the informatics sector is probably the most liberalized as both services and products are traded internationally. By contrast, the media and broadcasting sector has both highly internationalized elements and strongly protected national media companies. In part this is due to the cultural and political aspects of media products. The provision of information and cultural material is partially a public good that without state intervention may not be supplied to the general public. Thus states have sought to offer public broadcasting services and resisted liberalization of broadcasting. At the same time, the emergence of cable and satellite digital television has created a highly internationalized market for broadcasting alongside national broadcasting.

Somewhere between the media and informatics sector lie telecommunications services. Historically, telecommunications services were provided by a state monopoly. The service range offered was narrow and expensive. However, because certain sections of society, i.e. those residing in 'uneconomic' segments of the market, would not receive telecommunications provision, the state was obliged to provide service to these groups, cross-subsidizing these loss-making services by over-charging business and long-distance customers. As state-owned telecom providers faced soft budget constraints, they were frequently loss-making entities that required subsidies from taxpayers. Again, this situation was part of a legitimate political process in which societies in West Europe and North America agreed to maintain the status quo believing in a public service aspect to telecommunications services. This also took place at a time in which, arguably, the 'tele-formatics' revolution had yet to take place.

The situation in East and Central Europe prior to 1989 was a somewhat different situation. State control of industry and central planning meant that there was no serious discussion of liberalization of the telecommunications sector. As we note below, the level of service provision was markedly lower than in the market political economies of West Europe and North America. There was technological stagnation in the sector where waiting time to acquire a basic telephone line ran into years. The physical infrastructure was poor and selective. Thus, areas linked to the military-industrial complex received preferential access to telecommunications services and a large urban–rural split emerged in the supply of these services.

Thus while the situation in OECD countries before 1989 was arguably not optimal, the political economies of East and Central Europe were in an even worse condition.

By the 1990s, pressures from technological change in the sector created an unstoppable momentum for liberalization in the sector. Led by the privatization of telecommunications sectors in the 1980s in the US and UK, West European states began to privatize their telecommunications sectors. This was in part also due to the political imperative and momentum created by EU integration in which privatization was part of the narrative of liberalization and greater competition. The Reagan and Thatcher governments believed that in privatizing the telecommunications sectors, they could reduce state subsidies and create competitive forces to enhance technological change in the industry. Whether these decisions were due to prescient understanding of technological change in the industry or driven by the ideological dogma of free markets, once the US and UK sectors had become liberalized it was unlikely that West European telecommunications sectors would be able to resist for much longer.

The collapse of state planning in 1989 in East and Central Europe was the final ingredient in the liberalization recipe. Faced with no other option, states in the region were forced to privatize their telecommunications sectors. Different political economies took different paths: mass voucher privatization, creation of national, private entities or sales to strategic foreign investors.

As with West Europe, there was a need for regulatory models. Again, political economies took different paths. EU accession, however, provided an important yardstick for regulation and the EU liberalization model proved to be a tractable template for regulation and reform. Once again, the UK model of liberalization served as an imperfect exemplar for other countries in this context.

The central challenge in liberalizing telecommunications services is to recognize that competition is probably the most effective way of achieving greater choice for consumers. However, given the high level of R&D and infrastructure costs associated with the provision of telecommunications services, some degree of latitude on the number and scale of competitors has to be considered by regulators. On the one hand, the maintenance of near-monopoly control of telecommunications services is bound to lead to poorer service and higher prices in the absence of regulation, e.g. RPI-X. However, given the substantial fixed and sunk costs of investment in telecommunications networks, there is no guarantee that a network will be provided if firms are required to compete with each other. Thus the basic approach taken by regulatory authorities has been to grant the former PTOs a limited period of monopoly service provision followed by the introduction of competition in fixed-line telephony. In other sectors of telecommunications services, of course, competition emerged as a direct consequence of the fact that these sectors were new and developed after liberalization. Examples of these are mobile telephony and Internet services. Thus there was no need for price regulation as with fixed-line telephony. Once again, the Hungarian government took this route in its privatization and liberalization strategy. We now turn to the experience of Hungary's telecommunications sector.

8.3 Telecommunications in Hungary

In the period 1949–88, telecommunications services in Hungary, in common with other centrally planned political economies, were poor and little attention was paid to the development of infrastructure. As late as 1988, telephone density in Hungary was as low as 8.1 lines per 100 inhabitants or 25 per cent of the EU average.[2] There was as much as thirteen years of waiting time for a telephone line and no mobile telephony existed.[3] The Hungarian PTT was both supplier and regulator and no market existed for telecommunications services.

With the collapse of state planning and the resignation of the socialist government, one of the first steps taken by the new post-socialist government was to break up the Hungarian PTT into three separate entities: Magyar Posta (postal services), Antenna Hungaria (broadcasting) and MATÁV (telecommunications services). Second, the state separated regulatory and operational functions and created two new agencies to regulate the sector: the Postal and

Telecommunications Inspectorate and the Frequency Management Institute.

The development of telecommunications since 1989 in Hungary has been significant. It has produced an annual double-digit growth in the decade since 1989, far exceeding the growth rate of GDP. In 1999, sectoral volume was valued at 850bn forint ($3bn).[4] Investment in the sector has been impressive both in absolute and relative terms. Between 1994 and 1998, the average annual level of investment in the industry was 160bn forint ($600 mn). In 1999, the total figure for investment that year exceeded 204bn forint ($700mn).[5] In 1999 and projected figures for 2000 suggest that investment in telecommunications is around 8.5 per cent of total investment in the entire economy.[6] As an illustration of the importance of investment and of FDI in the telecommunications sector, MATÁV has invested $1.68 billion in the industry between 1999 and 2001.[7] Tables 8.1–8.3 illustrate the rapid growth of the sector since 1995.

Public consumption of telecommunications has experienced a considerable increase. Compared to the mid-90s, consumers spent

Table 8.1 Total income of the telecommunications sector (billion HUF)

	1996	1997	1998	1999
Postal services	75.1	97.6	98.7	118.4
Courier services	2.2	3.0	6.5	5.0
Telecommunications and broadcasting	281.0	399.3	538.8	728.4
Total	**358.3**	**499.9**	**644.0**	**851.8**

Source: Hungarian Central Statistical Office (KHVM).

Table 8.2 Trading profit of the telecommunications sector (billion HUF)

	1996	1997	1998	1999
Postal services	1.2	3.8	4.1	2.2
Courier services	0.1	0.1	0.2	0.3
Telecommunications and broadcasting	38.0	65.9	97.3	138.7
Total	**39.3**	**69.8**	**101.6**	**141.2**

Source: Hungarian Central Statistical Office (KHVM).

Table 8.3   Investments in the telecommunications sector (billion HUF)

	1996	1997	1998	1999
Postal services	3.9	6.2	8.5	11.9
Courier services	–	0.1	0.1	0.0
Telecommunications and broadcasting	106.7	142.7	141.9	192.5
Total	110.6	149.0	150.5	204.4

Source: Hungarian Central Statistical Office (KHVM).

one and a half more times income on telecommunications in 1999.[8] In turn, industry profitability has risen considerably. Between 1995 and 1998, operating profits rose from 12 billion forint to 97 billion forint ($40 million to $300 million). Table 8.4 details the operating figures of the main telecommunications companies.

Industry profitability is related to productivity growth in the industry. Both fixed-line and mobile telephony sectors have experienced growth in productivity measured in two ways: employees per 100 subscribers and subscribers per employee. Between 1997 and 1999, on the basis of the first measure, fixed-line productivity has increased (from 5.7 workers per 100 subscribers to 4) whereas mobile telephony has seen a decline in workers per 100 subscribers from 2.7 in 1997 to 1.5 in 1999. On the basis of the second measure, fixed-line telecommunications has seen an increase of subscribers per employee of 176 in 1997 to 249 in 1999. Growth in the mobile telephone sector has been spectacular: in 1997 there were 366 subscribers per worker, by 1999 that figure had reached 662.[9]

It is important to note the relative 'under-performance' of the fixed-line sector compared to the mobile sector. This could be explained by two principal factors. First is the relative market saturation of fixed-line telephony. Second, the quasi-monopoly position on MATÁV in fixed-line, local, national and long-distance telephony probably has held back productivity relative to other sectors of the telecommunications industry.

8.3.1 Fixed-line telephony

Until 1993, MATÁV remained 100 per cent state-owned but with the introduction of the Telecommunications Act (July 1993), the

Table 8.4 Main operating figures for telecommunications companies in Hungary (in HUF '000)

	Turnover		Trading profit		Retained profit	
	1998	*1999*	*1998*	*1999*	*1998*	*1999*
MATÁV	243 374 395	287 015 354	59 662 812	74 033 384	43 202 346	49 037 584
Vivendi	9 577 481	11 106 555	1 795 396	2 477 398	–9 631	1 911 466
Déltáv	7 138 179	8 282 774	558 115	1 211 526	–1 532 966	597 999
Digitel 2002	1 599 504	1 778 858	–52 773	230 305	–164 818	280 295
Jásztel	5 188 211	6 480 609	494 518	1 810 410	–1 336 679	1 089 921
Bakonytel	2 826 146	3 284 694	257 855	983 564	–886 046	359 568
Dunatel	1 956 825	2 255 667	66 215	532 123	–894 807	185 982
Egom-com	2 464 446	3 057 456	352 420	1 001 036	–334 791	673 572
Kisduna-com						
HTTC Pápatel	1 059 904	1 260 065	224 732	–186 721	–11 157 099	–1 056 040
Rábacom	1 218 031	1 505 678	125 680	136 284	–1 009 004	–899 862
Hungarotel	6 569 152	7 675 661	1 394 499	2 136 094	–2 786 481	–1 286 404
Kelet-Nógrad Com	2 475 106	3 001 748	571 362	840 967	–2 876 481	–1 286 404
MONOR	4 856 667	5 787 060	1 344 696	1 640 792	–664 852	278 613
EMITEL	5 204 191	5 988 398	960 179	1 953 022	468 192	1 378 779
Fixed operators	**295 508 238**	**348 480 577**	**67 755 846**	**88 800 184**	**31 846 474**	**51 830 412**
Pannon GSM	61 189 400	79 028 800	5 938 596	17 762 898	–839 549	12 668 294
Westel 450	14 726 600	14 124 100	1 286 959	1 492 710	0	0

Table 8.4 (Continued)

	Turnover		Trading profit		Retained profit	
	1998	1999	1998	1999	1998	1999
Westel 900	78 491 600	108 703 700	19 990 664	33 147 510	0	24 206 319
Vodafone	–	475 084	-310 198	-5 840 931	-260 287	-6 929 018
All Mobile	154 407 600	203 331 684	26 906 021	46 562 187	-1 099 836	29 945 595
Easycall	268 964	–	-226 739	-40 930	-1 160 103	-40 930
Eurohivó	170 843	169 770	-205 436	-61 965	-225 367	-46 975
Grand Total	450 355 645	551 982 031	94 229 692	135 259 476	29 361 168	81 688 102

Source: Hírközlési Főfelügyelet, 'Telecommunications in Hungary at the millennium': 8.

ground was set for the privatization of the company. The key aspect of the Act was to create the principle of concession and competitive services. Concession services included public voice telephony, public mobile telephony and nationwide distribution and broadcasting radio and TV. Competitive services included new emerging services such as data communication services that remained hitherto underdeveloped. On 22 December 1993, a consortium called MagyarCom, owned jointly by Deutsche Telekom and Ameritech won the contract to the national concession for twenty-five years and acquired 30.2 per cent of the shares of MATÁV Rt (joint stock company). It cost the consortium $875 million. This contract effectively granted a monopoly to MATÁV in the provision of national and international telephone services for eight years. MATÁV, the most valuable company of the ECE region, is the only regional telecommunications company with shares listed on the international stock exchanges, including the NYSE (from 1997). It is the biggest investor of the region and the only telecommunications company with no waiting list for the installation of new telephone lines (down from the 718 500 people waiting for lines in 1994).

In February 1994, the regional concession tenders were offered in order to create local telephone operators (LTOs). A total of fifty-four areas were created for the purposes of the tender (see Table 8.5).

MATÁV gained thirty-six of the total LTO contracts thus granting it 70 per cent of the land area of Hungary and 72 per cent of the population. Of the remaining LTO contracts, two foreign companies gained the majority: Vivendi Telecom (France) with nine LTOs and HTCC (US) with five contracts, and two small companies Emitel Rt and Monortel Rt gained the remainder. Vivendi currently has approximately 12 per cent of the market and is regarded as MATÁV's main competitor in light of market liberalization from 2002.[10] Vivendi has invested $600 million (677.4 million euros) so far. Vivendi currently serves some 80 000 customers with a staff of 1500 people through a regional network of LTOs.

A second round of privatization allowed MagyarCom to become the majority owner of MATÁV in December 1995, the consortium increasing their stake in the company to over 60 per cent at a cost of $852 million. The two rounds of privatization ensured that the sale of the Hungarian telecommunications provider would be the largest privatization in the region to date and the largest single foreign investment in Hungary.

Table 8.5   Local telephone operators in Hungary

Number	Name	Operator
1	Budapest	Matav Rt
2	Pecs	Matav Rt
3	Mohacs	Matav Rt
4	Szigetvar	Matav Rt
5	Kecskemet	Matav Rt
11	Miskolc	Matav Rt
12	Kazincbarcika	Matav Rt
13	Mezokovesd	Matav Rt
14	Szerencs	Matav Rt
17	Szekesfehervar	Matav Rt
19	Gyor	Matav Rt
20	Sopron	Matav Rt
21	Debrecen	Matav Rt
22	Berettyoujfalu	Matav Rt
23	Eger	Matav Rt
24	Gyongyos	Matav Rt
25	Szolnok	Matav Rt
27	Karcag	Matav Rt
28	Tatabanya	Matav Rt
31	Balassagyarmat	Matav Rt
32	Biatorbagy	Matav Rt
33	Cegled	Matav Rt
36	Szentendre	Matav Rt
39	Kaposvar	Matav Rt
40	Marcali	Matav Rt
41	Siofok	Matav Rt
42	Nyiregyhaza	Matav Rt
43	Kisvarda	Matav Rt
44	Mateszalka	Matav Rt
45	Szekszard	Matav Rt
46	Paks	Matav Rt
47	Szombathely	Matav Rt
51	Tapolca	Matav Rt
52	Zalaegerszeg	Matav Rt
53	Keszthely	Matav Rt
54	Nagykanizsa	Matav Rt
15	Szeged	Vivendi
16	Szentes	Vivendi
18	Dunaujvaros	Vivendi
26	Jaszbereny	Vivendi
29	Esztergom	Vivendi
34	Godollo	Vivendi

Table 8.5   (*Continued*)

38	Vac	Vivendi
37	Szigetszentmiklos	Vivendi
49	Veszprem	Vivendi
9	Bekescsaba	HTCC
10	Oroshaza	HTCC
30	Salgotarjan	HTCC
50	Papa	HTCC
48	Sarvar	HTCC
6	Baja	Emitel Rt
7	Kiskoros	Emitel Rt
8	Kiskunhalas	Emitel Rt
35	Monor	Monortel Rt

Source: Hírközlési Föfelügyelet, 'Telecommunications in Hungary at the millennium': 16.

Twenty-six per cent of MATÁV's remaining shares were publicly floated on the Budapest and New York Stock Exchanges and the Hungarian state maintained a 'golden share'.

In July 2000, Ameritech's successor company, SBC Communications, decided to opt out of the Hungarian telecommunications sector and sold its share of the MagyarCom consortium to Deutsche Telekom AG (the new privatized entity) for a market value of $4 billion (as of 30 June 2000). This meant that Deutsche Telekom now became the majority owner of the shares of the company (59.53 per cent) with the remaining shares being publicly traded.

8.3.2 Mobile telephony

Unlike fixed-line telephony, the mobile telephone sector can be characterized as being competitive with a higher current growth rate and higher potential growth rate. The main companies in the Hungarian sector are Westel 900 GSM, owned by MATÁV, Pannon GSM, owned by Telenor[11] and Vodafone, owned by a consortium led by Vodafone Airtouch, the world's largest mobile telephone company.[12] Once again, foreign ownership is significant in this sector of the industry, foreign firms being attracted by the attractive growth potential of the market.

The increase of the market in mobile telephone services has been spectacular. Total number of subscribers increased from the 1997 figure of 708 040 to over three million in 2000.[13] The market is effectively a duopoly with Westel GSM maintaining over 50 per cent market share and Pannon GSM controlling around 40 per cent of the market. The arrival of Vodafone and the relative decline of the Westel 450 analogue service have shifted the balance with Vodafone's market growth outstripping both Pannon and Westel (albeit from a low base).

By comparison with fixed-line services which appear to have reached close to saturation in Hungary, mobile service demand is increasing considerably faster. At the start of 1999, the proportion of mobile subscribers to fixed-line subscribers was 30 per cent. By the middle of 2000, that figure had reached 59 per cent.[14]

8.3.3 Data communications services

Outside of the concession-based services, data communications has developed largely outside of the framework of the 1993 Telecommunications Act. The most commonly used data communications services are leased line, ISDN and switched line services. The main type of end user is business with the domestic ISDN market being relatively underdeveloped. The main companies providing these services are once again foreign-owned companies: GTS Magyarorszag is 100 per cent owned by HTCC, Pantel is partly owned by KPN, Novacom is owned in the majority by RWE Telliance, and Telekommunikationsholding Sudwest GmbH and PartnerCom belong to Vivendi.

8.3.4 Internet services

Relative to other OECD economies, Hungary has the most expensive Internet services. This is largely due to the relatively high cost of telephone access rates. The average Internet user in Hungary spends 16 per cent of their monthly net salary on Internet services.[15] The main Internet Service Providers (ISPs) in Hungary are Axelero (formerly Matávnet), Elender, Datanet and Euroweb. Business use of Internet is mainly for the purposes of communication and promotion through website usage with e-commerce transactions being relatively low. This is primarily linked to the relatively low use of credit cards in Hungary as a means of payment in retail transactions.

The regulatory environment in Hungary as it relates to the Internet is at an early stage of development. Internet related issues are partly regulated by laws governing related technologies (i.e. telecom, media, etc.). Regulations on electronic documents and authentication of digital signatures are currently being drafted, with passage expected within two years.[16]

8.3.5 Cable television services

Almost 60 per cent of the total cable television market is owned by four large service providers, again mainly foreign-owned: UPC is the largest single firm with 550 000 subscribers in 1999; Matávkábeltv with 170 000 customers; Fibernet, owned by Prudential Insurance Company, with 100 000 clients; and EPA-HCS Kft with 50 000 subscribers. Current Hungarian legislation places a ceiling on the number of subscribers a company is allowed to have, i.e. 16 per cent of the population. With the coming into force of the new Communications Act (2001), there will be significant opportunities for cable television operators to link in the Internet and other telecommunications services to television services. As discussed in Section 8.1, the convergence of telecommunications technologies will offer the possibility for this to occur.

8.3.6 Terrestrial broadcasting

Of the three converging sectors, the media, and broadcasting in particular, remains somewhat underdeveloped in Hungary. Antenna Hungaria Rt (AH Rt) is the national surface television and radio company. As its market is already saturated, AH Rt is now increasing its presence in telecommunications sectors. It recently acquired 20 per cent in the Vodafone consortium.[17]

Table 8.5 provides a breakdown of the different telecommunications service providers (Sallai 1999: 13) by concession and non-concession contracts.

8.3.7 Public policy and the development of the telecommunications sector

Having outlined in detail the nature of the current Hungarian telecommunications sector, it is important to consider the role played by public policy in the development of the sector over the past twelve years. The official stated strategy of the Hungarian Communications Authority is that public policy has been based on four phases. The overall objective was to create an EU-level sector by not later than 2000.[18] Public policy in phase one, from 1990–3, was aimed at encouraging a digital infrastructure, i.e. updating the infrastructure inherited from the socialist era. In this phase, the government aimed to encourage more than 75 per cent of revenues to be directed towards investment in infrastructure. Phase two policy (1994–6) has prioritized a quantitative increase in the use of telecommunications services and a switch to full automization. This would allow the Hungarian telecommunications network to participate in pan-European and global networks. Phase three policy (1997–9) has been directed towards facilitating the growth of intelligent and business communication services and a reduction in the costs of telecommunications services. Since 2000, public policy has been geared towards the development of EU standard telecommunications services and achieving liberalization of the market.

As technologies in the sector have developed, public policy has developed simultaneously. Largely speaking, phases one and two public policy can be characterized as being based on technical licensing and supervision whereas phases three and four have emphasized market-based regulation with rules designed to ensure the fairness of free competition.

As discussed above, the first main public policy decision was to separate the operational and regulatory functions of telecommunications services. Act 72 of 1992, the first Telecommunications Act, created the concessions and competition-based distinction on services and created the conditions for the privatization of MATÁV. This Act was further strengthened in 1997 and 1999. These Acts have been supported by numerous related Acts and decrees.[19]

The Hungarian Communication Authority (HIF) is the licensing, supervisory, regulatory and administrative agency in Hungary which previously acted under the control of the Ministry for Transport, Communications and Water Management (KHVM). The HIF assisted the KHVM in the elaboration of acts, degrees and policy statements. Importantly for our study, the HIF monitors EU legislation concerning telecommunications and seeks to generate proposals for the harmonization of Hungarian laws to EU legislation. However, the Hungarian government has decided to shift political control of telecommunications policy from KHVM to the prime minister's office, suggesting the importance of this sector to the current leadership of the Hungarian government. It also begs questions about the independence and effectiveness of the regulatory role played by the HIF. It is arguable that liberalization of the sector is seen to bear significant political costs for the government and therefore it may attempt to control the independence of the process itself. To quote a recent policy document of the HIF:

Currently the most important task of HIF jointly with KHVM concerning law preparation is the elaboration of the new, unified Communications Act. This act ensures a unified, EU conform framework for fundamental rules on telecommunications, postal and information services [...] which is an essential aspect and pre-requisite for the accession of Hungary to EU.[20]

The Hungarian government had already introduced a number of EU-compliant laws in the field of liberalization. First, commercial voice telephony is allowed among closed user-groups. Second, LTOs are prohibited from imposing exclusive cable television rights in their areas of operation, thus creating the possibility for competition in the provision of cable television services. Third, all mobile telephone service providers have been granted equal access to 900 and 1800 MHz GSM frequency.[21]

8.3.8 Act 40 of 2001 on Communications

Prior to the introduction of the 2001 Communications Act, in October 2000, the EU Commission confirmed the efforts that Hungary had made in the area of telecommunications regulatory convergence. It noted that 'the telecommunications market, for example, was already closely aligned with the *acquis* and with the markets'.[22]

The Hungarian Parliament passed the new Communications Act referred to above in 2001. The Act, in full conformity with EU regulations and directives (outlined in article 109 of the new Act) created a uniform, market-based regulatory framework for telecommunications services in Hungary. The three most notable aims of the Act as outlined in article 2 are to ensure availability and free trade of communications services in accordance with international agreements including cross-border services, to promote the development of communications competition and to fulfil international obligations. These are central pillars of EU liberalization and directly reflect the requirements of regulatory convergence and harmonization that the Hungarian state must meet in order to join the EU. While the Act lists the EU legislation, the Act itself does not bring this legislation into force. Rather the Act is a framework which creates the necessary legal structures to allow for the promulgation of the various EU legislative instruments subsequently.[23] It is expected that some of the EU legislation will be introduced prior to accession while others will come into force on the day of accession.

Another important aspect of the Act is that MATÁV's position as concession holder comes to an end and its legal position changes. It is now a duty of MATÁV to provide loss-making services to remote areas rather than a right to provide services exclusively. Failure to provide services makes a company responsible for failure to meet its obligations – an important shift of burden for the company.[24]

The Act is nevertheless is a remarkable achievement. It has taken the Hungarian state a few years to develop an EU-conforming telecommunications framework that has taken two decades for existing member states to reach. While concerns about the independence of HIF from governmental pressure are valid, the framework itself is sound. As we will argue below, it is precisely the presence of foreign companies in the telecommunications sector that has aided this process.

8.4 Ownership structures in the Hungarian telecommunications sector

In this section we will examine the ownership and investment structures in the telecommunications sector. As our central argument aims to link ownership structures to legislative change, it is necessary to get an understanding of these structures.

In common with our other two case studies, the telecommunications sector in Hungary is predominantly foreign-owned. In fact ownership in the industry is almost exclusively foreign with the Hungarian state maintaining a 'golden share' in MATÁV. In the decade since privatization began, ownership of the industry has shifted as well. Initially, KPN telecom had a significant presence in the Hungarian sector but in recent times, in common with the Dutch banking compatriots ABN-AMRO and ING Bank, poor financial results have led to a withdrawal of their presence in Hungary.

8.4.1 MATÁV group

As discussed above MATÁV is the defining player in the Hungarian telecommunications sector. Owned in the majority by Deutsche Telekom, it has the lion's share of fixed-line telephony and owns Westel GSM, Hungary's largest mobile telephone company. Allegedly,

MATÁV was responsible for 40 per cent of Deutsche Telekom's total corporate profits in 2000.[25] In addition to the fixed-line and mobile business, MATÁV owns cable television interests, an ISP called Axelero and recently acquired a majority stake in the Macedonian telecommunications company Maktel.

Deutsche Telekom maintains a strong control of the company. The CEO is German. They have centralized a range of functions including treasury at headquarters in Germany. In this sense their strategy is similar to many MNEs based in Hungary.[26] There is some controversy related to the premature termination of MATÁV's concession exclusivity. Since introducing the new Communications Act required the liberalization of the telecommunications sector, it meant that the eight-year exclusivity as envisaged in the original concession contract was reduced to seven years. According to industry experts, MATÁV was compensated for this although the amount was never made public.[27]

In the first two phases of the Hungarian state's telecommunications strategy, Deutsche Telekom, *inter alia* MATÁV played a crucial role in upgrading the telecommunications infrastructure through significant investments. Unsurprisingly, the political and financial *quid pro quo* for these investments was the exclusive concession rights that the Hungarian state granted it.

8.4.2 Vivendi group

The second major grouping in the Hungarian telecommunications sector is the French-owned Vivendi group. The Vivendi group, then named Compagnie Générale Satellites et de Télévisions, established its first subsidiary in Hungary in April 1994.[28] After MATÁV, it has the largest network of LTOs. It has recently merged its various LTOs into one company called V-Fon Telecom Services.[29] It plans to merge all of its LTOs into this company eventually. V-Fon has also ventured into the ISP sector now providing nationwide ISP coverage. Industry analysts believe that Vivendi's aggressive investment strategy in the 1990s leaves it well placed to compete in the liberalized market after 2001.[30]

8.4.3 Other foreign companies

Hungarian Telephone and Cable Corporation (HTCC) was originally set up by a joint Danish and US venture. It owns four LTOs. Postabank recently acquired a 20 per cent stake in the company against loan repayments taken by the company. Monortel, owned by the Dutch company UPC, owns one LTO.

Pannon GSM is Hungary's second largest mobile service with around 30 per cent of the market in 2000. It launched its service in 1994 as a consortium of Swedish, Dutch, Danish and Hungarian companies. Ownership has changed hands since then with Telia (Sweden) and TeleDenmark selling their stake in the company. Most recently, Telenor (Norway) acquired a 100 per cent stake in the company paying 1.2bn Euros ($1bn) for the shares in July 2001.[31]

Vodafone, owned by a joint venture company VRAM Co, is mostly owned by the world's largest mobile phone company Vodafone Air-Touch Plc (50.1 per cent). Antenna Hungária owned a 20 per cent stake and Magyar Post has a 10 per cent share of the company. The reason for Hungarian ownership in Vodafone is that it is required by law under the concession agreement signed by VRAM Co whereby the Hungarian state stipulated a minimum 25 per cent ownership of the company. In April 2001, Antenna Hungária increased its share of Vodafone to 30 per cent.[32]

A similar pattern of ownership can be discerned in other, smaller telecommunications services ranging from paging to satellite telephony and ISPs.[33]

8.4.4 Equipment manufacturers

It is worth noting the presence in Hungary of the world's leading telecommunications equipment manufacturers, too. Their activities in Hungary are broad-based. Siemens (Germany), Ericsson (Sweden), Nokia (Finland), Panasonic (Japan) and Motorola (US) are all involved in the manufacture of telecommunications equipment in Hungary.

The Siemens group comprises around twenty companies with total revenue of 86 billion forint ($300 million) in 1999.[34] It was one of the original winners of the tenders to build main telephone exchanges in Hungary in 1989. Panasonic produces GSM telephones, fax machines, office equipment in Hungary, and in 2000 Panasonic Hungary had sales revenue of 40 billion forint ($135 million).[35] Ericsson Hungary Ltd has made a significant commitment to Hungarian telecommunications since its establishment in Hungary in December 1990. Most notable has been the setting of its European R&D headquarters in Budapest, taking advantage of Hungary's skilled mathematicians and computer scientists and some leading edge research at the Technical University of Budapest.

Nokia, the world's leading producer of mobile telephones, won the tender offered by Pannon GSM for the supply of its GSM network for its Nokia Networks subsidiary and a similar contract was signed with Vodafone in 1999.[36] Motorola produces mobile phones in three locations in Hungary: Zalaergerzeg, Budapest and Debrecen.

8.4.5 Future outlook

Given the current global trend in the telecommunications industry where mergers and acquisitions are becoming central to survival strategies for MNEs in the sector, the Hungarian industry, like any other in the global market, is likely to be affected. Given the large capital expenditure requirements for entering the Hungarian sector, it is likely that a global merger is likely to affect the Hungarian sector rather than specific events in Hungary causing consolidation and new entry. One of the most significant events took place in 2000 when the Hungarian state auctioned the 3.5 GHz bandwidth.[37] Once again, foreign firms were in the first line to win these bids. Notably, MATÁV and PanTel acquired frequency at the cost of 600 million forint ($2.2 million). V-Com acquired frequency at 50 million forint ($180 000). The frequency rights last for fifteen years but use of the frequency for voice communication would only be allowed after liberalization under the new Communications Act in 2002.[38]

8.5 The link between MNE presence and regulatory convergence

The role of MNEs in the Hungarian telecommunications sector has been crucial in bringing the sector up to date after the collapse of central planning in 1989. Forced by macroeconomic and budgetary pressures to pay off external debt, the Hungarian government sold key telecommunications companies to strategic foreign investors and in doing so raised badly needed money to repay the debt and found an important source of external capital. As telecommunications services FDI is largely of the market-seeking kind, it was reasonable to expect that MNE presence was likely to be reasonably long-lasting. The prospect of growing incomes in Hungary, regarded at the start of the transition process as being one of the CEE political economies with greatest economic growth potential, attracted foreign companies. The fact that Hungary was also one of the first of the CEE transition political economies to launch upon a wholesale privatization of state assets to strategic foreign investors granted Hungary 'first-mover advantage' over neighbouring states.

The aim of this section is to examine the indirect means by which MNEs in Hungary influenced the process of regulatory convergence in the telecommunications sector. Based on interviews with managers and policy-makers in the sector, what emerges adds further evidence for our claim that MNEs play a positive role in facilitating regulatory convergence.

Through significant investment in new technologies and in upgrading the existing fixed-line network, privatization of the sector led to a rapid advance of service provision and standards. Indeed, the relative speed with which competition was introduced in the new non-fixed line services significantly aided the development of new services especially in the fields of data transmission and, above all, in mobile telephony.

One industry observer expressed concern that although the new Communications Act has been introduced, bringing with it EU-compliant regulation, it is unlikely that full competition will arrive immediately as MATÁV's position is strong.[39] Moreover, the competition in services will focus initially mainly on large users of telecommunications services in the business sector.[40] Despite this, the progress made in Hungary is in stark contrast to the problems faced in the Czech telecommunications sector.[41]

MNE investment has probably been one of the main contributing factors to the success of implementation of the EU *acquis* in Hungary. Foreign ownership is so extensive that local competition (and hence resistance to liberalization) is minimal. While MATÁV had incentives to resist liberalization, its competitors in fixed-line services led by Vivendi have been preparing for competition with the monopoly incumbent. Moreover, competition from non-fixed-line services has undermined MATÁV's position in the business sector. As can be appreciated from the data examined above, the growth of fixed-line services is limited and thus MATÁV's position has to be extended into more competitive sectors such as mobile telephony.

8.6 Conclusions

Our final case study examined the telecommunications sector in Hungary. Like the banking and electricity sectors, a well-functioning and competitive telecommunications sector is vital to the development of a transition economy. It is a key technological infrastructure for industry and high-cost telecommunications services impact heavily on other sectors as the role of knowledge-based resources in industry rises and as effective communications across borders become central to the strategy of companies.

Historically, telecommunications services were the preserve of a state-owned monopoly. The UK and North American liberalization experiments led to a wholesale shift in the regulatory and public policy emphasis of telecommunications. As part of this change, EU member states began to privatize and liberalize their telecommunications sectors as part of a drive towards the creation of the EU single market in telecommunications services. Both anticipating and precipitating technological change, the liberalization process created a new industrial and competitive landscape across the EU. While privatized national telecommunications incumbents maintained dominant positions in fixed-line services, the growth of new telecommunications services enabled business and to a lesser degree consumer market segments to become increasingly competitive.

As part of joining the EU, candidate countries needed to undertake to implement the EU liberalization legislation. Hungary, as with many other sectors, has led the way among candidate countries with full implementation of the *acquis* in place with the coming into force of the new Communications Act of 2001. In our research for this case we have found, as with the banking and electricity sectors, the role of foreign ownership has been crucial in pushing the Hungarian sector towards liberalization. In manifest ways, new technologies, investment and managerial processes have led to the development of a competitive industry in most sectors. Of note is the growth of mobile telephony, frequently as an alternative to fixed-line services.

In some senses, the level of competition in the sector from the presence of MNEs is somewhere between the banking and electricity sectors. To the extent that MATÁV is still dominant in the fixed-line sector, the case resembles more the regional monopoly case of the electricity sector. However, the presence of a number of highly competitive non-fixed line sectors such as mobile telephony and Internet services means that MATÁV's position is not guaranteed as telephony can be provided using non-fixed line services.

This can partially explain the relatively rapid liberalization of the sector compared to the slower and more problematic implementation of EU liberalization directives in the electricity sector.

Industry observers and managers note that it will be interesting to see how quickly genuine competition will emerge on the back of the EU liberalization legislation. It is certain that without the implementation of the legislation concerned, the industry would not be competitive. The implementation itself, as we have hoped to demonstrate in our case, is due to the role of the MNE in the Hungarian sector.

9
Conclusions

9.1 Introduction

The starting point for our study was to examine two important processes in the world political economy. First, the conceptual and empirical realization that the MNE is an important political entity in the policy-making processes of states and international organizations. Second, the process of EU enlargement to include countries from ECE would entail one of the greatest projects in regulatory convergence; a process in which the transforming political economies of the ECE region would have to revolutionize their legal structure and substance and overhaul their system of public administration to fall in line with the *acquis*.

We have tried to draw a link between these two processes – the increasing influence of the MNE and the process of EU regulatory convergence – by arguing that the pursuit of competitive advantage by MNEs in international competition has the effect of driving up standards in certain key circumstances. These have been illustrated by examining the role of 'standards' competition in service industries in Hungary. One of the most important findings in our study is that where higher service standards are a key feature of competitive advantage for the MNE, there is an important relationship between the introduction of new legislation and the activities of MNEs. In particular, we have demonstrated that as frequently MNEs in Hungary come from the EU, they have sought to use EU standards that they themselves helped to formulate within the EU context, in their competitive struggles with local companies.

This has also had the desirable effect of forcing improvements in service provision among local companies as they have been forced to raise the quality of their service provision to compete with the foreign companies. Throughout our research, managers and administrators have remarked upon the profound impact that foreign companies have had on the regulatory and competitive structures in the industries we examined.

While raising standards to EU levels has improved quality of service and enhanced the process of regulatory convergence towards EU requirements, our story is not universally explanatory in two important ways. First, we have not examined manufacturing sectors where there could be different dynamics at work. In particular, it is possible to find that, in fact, MNEs may make use of lower product and production standards if the main purpose of their activity is to serve a local or regional non-EU market. On the contrary, if they are using the 'low-cost' base of ECE to produce for export to the EU, then they would be compelled to produce to EU standards.

Second, where there is no major regulatory imperative such as the adoption of the *acquis communautaire*, there is no guarantee that the use of higher standards by MNEs will necessarily be linked to the introduction of new legislation in the host countries. This latter point is crucially important for the normative implications of our work. We are not in any way claiming that our study provides a blue-print for the encouragement of FDI as a strategy for regulatory convergence in particular, or an economic development strategy in general. Under limited circumstances the features specific to Hungary could be repeated in other ECE political economies. However, we are at pains to emphasize the historical contingencies facing Hungary in 1989: high sovereign debt and a significant trade deficit forced Hungarian legislators to embark upon a significant privatization process based around foreign sales of Hungarian companies. Moreover, Hungary's geo-economic position and its relatively sound industrial base in a number of key sectors, proved to be attractive to MNEs. In addition, the favourable factor conditions in post-socialist Hungary, such as a relatively highly trained workforce, encouraged MNEs to choose Hungary as a location for Greenfield investment. These three factors were present before the arrival of FDI and were not a consequence of the decision to allow MNEs to invest in Hungary. Certainly, the activities of MNEs have contributed substantially to the upgrading of

Hungary's industrial landscape, but we are not suggesting that political economies that do not possess favourable geo-economic and supply-side conditions could definitely repeat Hungary's experience.

Nevertheless, the impact of the MNE in the sectors covered in our study has been profound. The aim of this concluding chapter is to provide a recap of our main findings in each of the sectors we examined, to draw these findings together more generally to develop some common results and, at the same time, understand key differences across the sectors. Second, we aim to offer some sector-specific and broader conclusions of our work. In particular, we aim to encourage further research into the issue of regulatory convergence and the MNE, and in setting additional research questions that arise from our findings, we hope to able to set up a research agenda for others to follow up.

Section one of this chapter provides a detailed summary of our results by sector: banking, electricity and telecommunications services respectively. Section two attempts to compare and contrast our findings across sectors enabling us to develop broader questions and implications based on our research. Section three sets a forward-looking research agenda. In this section, we aim to encourage further detailed study into this key relationship and its relevance for the European and world political economy.

9.2 Banking services

One of the first sectors to be liberalized and privatized was the banking sector. From a public finance perspective, the Hungarian government sought to liberalize in order to break the link between industry finance and state ownership. By moving from single-tier to a two-tier banking structure, the creation of private banks would allow for a more financially rational allocation of securities and assets across the sector. By separating the central bank from the second-tier commercial sector, the Hungarian government was attempting to create political distance between the central bank's monetary obligations and the pre-1989 political ties in industry. Of course, this objective wouldn't necessary always happen – the Czech banking sector has suffered from the absence of so-called 'hard budget constraints' and the numerous problems of bank financing in Russia attest to the weakness of the separation between the private banking sector and the central bank.

Nevertheless, the Hungarian state also recognized that in creating a private banking sector, the issuing of government bonds would create an additional means of financing its significant external debt, largely inherited after 1989.

These objectives: both to 'depoliticize' the financing of privatized industry and the creation of a new non-inflationary source of government financing were the backdrops to a significant transformation in the functioning of the banking sector which has allowed for the creation of EU-compliant banking practices that, in the words of a respected expert in transition political economy, has created only 'mildly problematic' conditions in just over a decade.[1]

So what are the main findings of our research into regulatory convergence in the Hungarian banking sector? In order to discuss these conclusions, we remind the reader of the development of the sector.

9.2.1 The development of the Hungarian banking sector

From 1989 onwards, the arrival of MNEs immediately created a need for an internationally competitive corporate banking sector, set up largely to meet the needs of the MNEs. A foreign consortium led by Banca Commerciale Italiana, Citibank and other smaller investors created the CIB Bank. Before the Hungarian law on foreign banks allowed the setting up of foreign subsidiaries, a number of foreign banks set up representative offices. As soon as the law was liberalized, a number of foreign banks made their entry into the market.[2] This coincided with the privatization of the banking sector and significant acquisitions were made including GE Capital's acquisition of Budapest Bank. Foreign entry also included Dutch banking MNEs ING and ABN-AMRO. Citibank also set up its own banking network at this time. Austrian banks, given the geographical proximity of the Hungarian sector, set up banking networks including Creditanstalt and Raffeisen Bank. Foreign and joint venture banks, such as CIB Bank (majority owned by Banca Commerciale Italiana Group), Bank Austria Creditanstalt (Austria), Raiffeisen (Austria) and Citibank (US) control around 35 per cent of total assets and are typically specialized in corporate banking.

Foreign participation in the Hungarian banking system is very high. Foreign banks hold controlling stakes in twenty-seven banks, and the total foreign ownership is around 60 per cent of the registered capital. Foreign investment greatly helped the modernization of many Hungarian middle-sized banks through the supply of know-how and capital the same year Magyar Kulkereskedelmi Bank (MKB) was purchased jointly by Bayerische Landesbank (Germany) and the EBRD. ABN-AMRO (Netherlands) bought Magyar Hitel Bank (MHB) in 1996.

The largest commercial bank, OTP Bank, the former state savings bank and the 'retail' arm of the single-tier centrally planned economy, rather than being sold to a strategic investor was held partly in state ownership with the remainder being floated on the emerging Budapest stock exchange. OTP offers a wide range of complimentary products through its subsidiaries, which include OTP Real Estate (real estate management), OTP Building Society, OTP Securities (stock brokerage), OTP Confidencia (pension fund) and OTP Garancia (insurance). As OTP does not have a strategic foreign majority owner, it makes it unique among the large Hungarian banks. OTP's gradual privatization was conducted through the stock exchange and its shares are held by foreign and domestic institutional and portfolio investors. In 1999, the state sold its remaining stake in OTP through a secondary offering, but kept a golden share.

A number of key steps taken by the Hungarian state ensured that OTP's position in the retail sector would remain dominant. These included the requirement that all civil servants would have their salaries paid directly into a bank account which would be held at OTP. Given the nature of switching costs facing small retail banking customers, this immediately created a captive market which foreign banks would find difficult to break down.[3] Second, the state itself would continue politically to support the development of OTP, regarding it as a 'national champion'. One of the most notable attempts to support OTP was its attempt to encourage a takeover of the indebted and ailing Postabank.[4] In taking over Postabank, it would have granted OTP almost 80 per cent market share in the retail sector and would have resolved Postabank's indebtedness without the need for a politically explosive debt write-off. Postabank, the postal savings bank, was a severely indebted financial entity. The vast majority of its account holders were pensioners and thus the prospect of hundreds of thousands of poor pensioners losing their savings would prove too risky politically for any party in the Hungarian political system.

Thus, by the mid-1990s, the Hungarian banking sector could be characterized by a retail sector dominated by OTP and Postabank with only Budapest Bank, K&H Bank and ABN-AMRO as having sufficient scale in the retail sector in order to compete. Indeed, soon after their 'Greenfield' entry into the retail sector, ING Bank decided to close down its retail operations having failed to achieve sufficient scale to reduce costs.[5] This was further underlined by the decision of K&H and ABN-AMRO to merge their retail operations. Akbar and McBride (2002) argue that while foreign banks have played a positive role in several ways, they have not really encouraged the development of a flourishing personal lending and mortgage sector. This is largely due to the fact that the costs of this kind of financial service in a transition economy are relatively high. Second, low income levels and a conservative attitude to borrowing among Hungarian customers have held back demand for these services.

By contrast, in the corporate sector the picture was significantly different with a number of foreign banks competing vigorously for MNE customers and the emerging Hungarian-owned industrial sector. A number of niches in key sectors allowed foreign banks to serve their foreign clients without the need for large infrastructure.[6] Moreover, national preference among MNEs remains important with MNEs choosing banks of the same nationality as their principal bank.

Nevertheless, the presence of foreign banks in the sector has improved the overall functioning of the banking sector and has created the threat of competition in the retail sector for OTP Bank.

9.2.2 The regulatory environment

On the regulatory side, the Hungarian negotiators had closed the Financial Services chapter of the negotiations by 2001 and this is in part due to the fact that the main raft of EU legislation required for EU conformity had already been introduced by 1998. This included the framework Second Banking Directive as well as related legislation such as capital adequacy.

The relative speed with which Hungarian legislators had been able to introduce and implement EU rules has been aided in great part by the role played by foreign banks and the competitive game based around higher standards played by the market participants themselves. Arguably, one of the main competitive advantages that foreign banks possessed over their domestic rivals was an ability to offer higher and safer services standards because of their considerable experience of operating in the EU. Leveraging this competitive advantage implied basing their competitive strategy around higher standards (rather than price – a traditional competitive weapon). This strategy pervaded all operational aspects of their businesses from marketing to capital structure.

Local banks faced the choice of either losing market share to the foreign banks in the corporate and retail sector (although less so in the latter) or raising their standards to meet the foreign banks. The net result of this process was an overall upgrading of service standards in the industry. As for regulatory convergence, the adjustment costs associated with a move towards higher standards in the industry were not so great for two reasons. First, the banking sector was already held in the main by foreign banks operating to EU standards anyway. Second, OTP Bank had already gone some way to raising its own standards to fend off competition. This meant that the political resistance to change was lower which, in turn, enabled legislators to introduce the EU legislation in a relatively short period of time. This result was a remarkable one. In less than a decade, the Hungarian banking sector had been transformed into an internationally rated sector thanks in great measure to the need of the Hungarian state to sell domestic banks to foreign companies to pay sovereign debt obligations.

In selling Hungary's banks to strategic foreign investors, the process of regulatory convergence was started which today means that Hungary's banking sector is on the verge of being part of the EU banking sector upon Hungary's accession. Whether further structural transformations take place upon accession is unclear. The fact that Hungary's bank balance sheets are relatively healthy suggests that they could be the target for further acquisition.

9.3 Electricity

Alongside financial services as a key infrastructural sector, a functioning energy sector is crucial in the successful economic development of a transition political economy. In Chapter 7, we examined the development of the electricity sector in Hungary and the extent to which the Hungarian state had successfully implemented EU energy sector liberalization directives. Moreover, as with the banking case study, we sought to gauge the extent to which foreign ownership in the electricity sector had facilitated this process. Like the banking case study, foreign ownership in the electricity sector is extensive (although not to the same degree as banking). There are three key sub-sectors to consider: electricity generation, electrical power transformation and electricity distribution. The following two sections will examine first market structure and then the process of regulatory convergence in the sector.

9.3.1 Market structure and foreign ownership

Privatization of the electricity sector has been the defining feature in the structural transformation of the electricity sector in Hungary. Along the lines of a UK model of privatization, the Hungarian state decided to sell regional distribution monopolies to strategic investors. On the generation side, there was also separate privatization of different generating companies producing electricity from a range of sources (coal, gas, lignite, etc.). An innovation undertaken by the government was to create a central transforming company called MVM Rt that remained largely in state ownership. This company bought the electricity at administered prices from the generating companies and sold the electricity to the distribution companies at regulated prices. The aim of this policy was to ensure that neither the generation nor distributing companies could charge 'uneconomical' prices to consumers.

It was also an interim measure prior to market liberalization under the terms of EU electricity liberalization directives. The new Electricity Act now allows for partial liberalization in which large companies can choose their supplier of electricity. MVM Rt has been broken up into MVM and MAVIR in order to avoid the problem of the state-owned entity being both a supplier of electricity and a maintenance function of the national grid, the latter taking over control of the grid.

Foreign ownership of the electricity sector is widespread with all of the distributing companies being sold to strategic foreign investors and virtually all of the electricity generating plants being sold to foreign companies. Notably, the Paks Nuclear Power Station has not been sold and remains in state control. However, the main MNEs in the electricity sector are RWE and E.ON of Germany, EDF of France, Tractabel of Belgium and Powergen of the UK. All of these companies have made substantial investments in plant and capital infrastructure and have transformed the Hungarian electricity sector from being a highly inefficient, environmentally hazardous and over-employed sector into one of the leading electricity sectors in the ECE region. As we discuss below, this has had a substantial positive effect on the ability of the Hungarian state to implement EU-compliant legislation.

One area of concern has been the signing of long-term contracts which was the original 'sweetener' for MNEs to invest in the first instance. As pressures for liberalization along the lines of EU legislation have increased, there has been controversy over the reneging of contracts. Some of the newly privatized companies have asked to be compensated for this. At the time of writing, the issue had not been fully resolved.

Most managers and regulators expect that as competition in the sector intensifies after liberalization, there will be consolidation among the main firms in the industry. This replicates the experience of most other West European markets. One of the positive benefits of FDI in the sector has been the 'internationalization' or 'Europeanization' of the sector with the companies now having access to a wider network of energy companies and wider sources of energy and finance.

9.3.2 Regulatory convergence and FDI

In the banking sector, competition based on higher service standards has been one of the main contributory factors to the speed with which the Hungarian state has been able to implement the EU-compliant legislation. By contrast, we have found that competition based on service standards has not been the main contributory factor in raising regulatory standards towards EU levels and preparing the Hungarian electricity sector for liberalization. Rather, two main factors can be cited for explaining the contribution of FDI to the process of regulatory convergence. First, it has been the role played by injections of foreign capital into the industrial infrastructure that has prepared the industry for competition. Second, the introduction of Western management techniques and processes in the electricity sector has been a significant factor in improving the ability of privatized companies to raise their production and service standards.

Managers and regulators in the industry, while not being whole-heartedly in praise of the role of foreign companies in the sector, have nevertheless remarked upon the generally positive role played by foreign ownership. This less than glowing assessment of foreign companies is due in part to the problems of introducing competition into the industry while encouraging foreign companies to invest in new capital. The trade-off was resolved by the granting of exclusive supply contracts to distributors of electricity for a limited period before competition would be introduced – essentially a period of time to allow for them to recoup their capital investment.

Nevertheless, the role played by foreign companies in the improvement of environmental and safety standards in the industry has been crucial in pushing the sector towards EU compliance. Due to the environmentally hazardous nature of state socialist energy production, the MNEs who acquired the plant and network had to undertake significant environmental clean-up costing millions of US$. This largely successful clean-up has ensured that Hungary complies with virtually all EU legislation concerning environmental protection in the electricity sector. Hungarian health and safety officials regard some of the practices at the electricity sectors as benchmark best practice and they comply with EU health and safety standards. Lastly, the role of human resource management has been applauded by the EU and Hungarian government as the painful restructuring of the sector has led to significant job losses across the sector with employment shrinking considerably in the generation side of the electricity sector.

The EBRD has described the Hungarian electricity sector reforms as far-reaching and radical. Indeed, if the objective of the architects of liberalization and privatization was to achieve EU-level standards of generation and supply, they have, on paper at least, produced a regulatory framework that is compliant with EU standards. While concerns still remain over the role of MVM and MAVIR and the strong relationship to government, our research in the sector suggests that a significant, if not complete, step has been made in the sector towards EU membership.

9.4 Telecommunications

In our third case study, the role of foreign ownership of the sector has also been pervasive and profound. In privatizing the Hungarian telecommunications sector and selling it to strategic foreign investors, the Hungarian state was trying to achieve three objectives. First, was to improve the infrastructure of the telecommunications network that seriously lagged behind West European standards. Second, it was trying to achieve a balance between incentives for a foreign investor and the development of competition in the sector, and third, it would use the funds raised to contribute towards paying off its foreign debt obligations.

While it is not clear which of these three objectives was the most important for the Hungarian government, the first two objectives involved a trade-off. On the one hand, the sector desperately needed investment in infrastructure because of the lack of investment under the socialist system. If a foreign investor were to be persuaded to undertake such an investment, it would need certain guarantees that for a given period of time it would be able to recoup its investment. On the other hand, part of a transition towards a market economy implied the development of competitive forces in industry. In the telecommunications sector, this implied the need to introduce competitors into the Hungarian sector.

As FDI in this sector has been predominantly market-serving, it is reasonable to suggest that foreign companies are likely to remain engaged in the sector as rising Hungarian incomes are likely to lead to increased demand for telecommunications services in the medium to longer term.

9.4.1 Market structure and foreign ownership

The choice made by the Hungarian state was to grant MATÁV an eight-year monopoly to supply fixed-line telephone services on a national and international basis. In addition, nearly forty LTOs were created to supply local call networks and MATÁV gained the majority of those. Since MATÁV was going to undertake the lion's share of investment in infrastructure in the sector, the *quid pro quo* for this was to offer a monopoly for a restricted period of time. Thus, the costs to consumers of having a monopoly supplier involved probably higher prices for telecommunications services than under a situation of competition. However, the sector received the necessary infrastructural upgrading. MATÁV's monopoly ended on 23 December 2001.

As the telecommunications sector encompasses not just fixed-line telephony, but also a range of other services such as mobile telephony, satellite television and Internet services, the role of foreign companies in Hungary has been equally extensive in these areas. For example, the three mobile telephone service providers – Westel, Pannon and Vodafone – are all partially or completely foreign-owned: in Westel's case it is owned by a consortium led by Deutsche Telekom (owners of

MATÁV); Pannon is owned now by Telenor and Vodafone by the world's largest mobile telephone services company Vodafone Airtouch. In the Internet sector, Hungary's largest supplier, Axelero, is owned by MATÁV and the management is appointed by Deutsche Telekom.

The other significant foreign company present in Hungary is Vivendi Telecom of France. It has an important share of the LTOs and according to industry observers is likely to emerge as Deutsche Telekom's main rival in the Hungarian telecommunications sector. It has made significant investments in infrastructure and is therefore expected to be a patient investor in the light of the end of MATÁV's monopoly.

9.4.2 Regulatory convergence and FDI

How has foreign ownership in the Hungarian telecommunications sector affected the process of regulatory convergence? In our research we have found that the role of the foreign company has not been the leveraging of competitive advantage as in the case of the banking sector. Instead, the significant investment in physical infrastructure and capital has played an important role in the creation of a sector that has been modernized and prepared for liberalization and competition. While actual competition has not been the principal driving force, potential competition, embodied in the limited eight-year exclusivity contract signed by MATÁV, has required Deutsche Telekom to prepare for competition. Upgrading in infrastructure and the range of services has been part of their competitive strategy in preparation for liberalization. This has meant that, in anticipating future competition, MATÁV has placed itself in a strong position ahead of competition.[7]

Moreover in other sub-sectors of the telecommunications industry, competition has been vigorous in Hungary with the mobile telephone sector being a leading example of this.

The new Communications Act, introduced in December 2001, is fully compliant with EU liberalization directives in the telecommunications sector. The EU Commission's own 'screening' of the sector suggests that Hungarian regulators have been able to implement legislation preparing Hungary for EU membership. There is little doubt among those in industry and government that the role of foreign companies has been crucial in dragging the sector up to EU standards.

9.5 Policy-making implications

In addition to conceptually and empirically developing an important phenomenon of the impact of MNE activity on the regulatory structures of political economies, our study also aims to generate some policy-making implications for interested industry managers, regulators and policy-makers.

First and foremost, it is vital to emphasize that our policy-making implications do not offer a *carte blanche* or a menu for policy-makers and industry managers. Rather, on the basis of our three, detailed case studies, we feel confident that we can offer some insights into the policy-making and strategy process. This section aims to offer these findings and draws some tentative conclusions.

In order to proceed, we feel it is necessary to make explicit our assumptions behind our suggestions. First, we assume that domestic industries are an attractive proposition for FDI and assets and market potential can be valued by MNEs. This is especially the case when we are dealing with privatization given the difficulties in valuing state assets in transition political economies. Second, we limit our suggestions to the impact on regulatory convergence and make no claims about the long-term impact of foreign ownership of industry and sovereignty issues that accompany this. Third, the effects that we have examined are appropriate when a state is seeking to raise regulatory standards to align with an international agreement or another country.

Perhaps our strongest finding is the role played by competition among MNEs and with local companies in service sectors that drives standards upwards. In all three sectors, but especially banking, we found that it is vigorous competition in standards that has raised the quality of service provision in the sectors we examined. This has meant that the rules of entry to the market have implied that in order to survive, new entrants have to offer high standards at least at the level of existing companies. This has radically changed the competitive landscape of the industries concerned and thus the political pressure of protection of domestic industrial interests has been reduced. In particular, the legislative process of introducing new legislation has been made smoother because industrial standards are already at EU levels and thus both workers and owners in the industries are already prepared for the new liberalized industrial regimes.

For policy-makers, the central implication is that MNE entry in service sectors can be a powerful aid in raising regulatory standards in industry – especially if this is part of a larger process of regulatory convergence towards international or regional standards such as joining the EU. Making MNE entry more attractive in this sense is a policy implication of this first finding. How states can facilitate MNE entry is a much broader public policy issue but can involve a range of incentives from fiscal policy (e.g. tax breaks) to infrastructural support (e.g. improving transport links). More generally, it involves a change of 'attitude' towards MNEs in terms of regulatory approaches. This is beyond the scope of our study. However, the Hungarian state has offered some of the most 'MNE friendly' conditions such as an attractive fiscal regime and minimization of bureaucratic procedures. Critics of this policy have claimed that the Hungarian state has sold the Hungarian political economy to foreigners and that it has long-term negative impacts on domestic capital accumulation. This is not an issue we have sought to address and it is beyond the scope of our study.

Our second finding is that MNEs can substantially improve the material and industrial infrastructure of the political economies in which they operate. Clearly, the objective of this FDI is for commercial returns but given the external 'spillovers' involved in investment in network industries such as telecommunications and energy, the upgrading of the infrastructure enables the development of quality service provision in these industries thus meeting international standards (and in our study EU standards). This creates new economic opportunities for companies supplying the MNEs and even should the MNE exit the market in the medium to longer term, the infrastructure itself remains intact. From the perspective of the policy-maker, improved infrastructure allows for the provision of EU-compliant services which, in turn facilitates the introduction of legislation that is compliant with EU standards.

The third main policy-making implication of our study is that actual or potential competition is an essential feature of allowing MNE entry to exert the greatest potential regulatory effects. A foreign firm, as with a local firm, is unlikely to pursue higher, often more costly, standards if there is no threat that 'under-performance' will be met with new entry.[8] Thus in two cases we have examined – telecommunications and electricity – there has been an issue of striking the correct balance between offering a limited period of monopoly or exclusivity for the MNE to reap returns on their investments in infrastructure and the need to improve service standards in the medium to long term. Thus Hungarian policy-makers were keen to ensure that MNEs were aware that in the medium term, competition was a key aim of the regulators. In the banking sector we examined in Chapter 6, although OTP maintains a lion's share of the retail banking sector, its position in the corporate sector is weak compared to their foreign counterparts and, almost as importantly, OTP recognizes that without a substantial improvement in the services it provides, the presence of foreign competitors represents a threat to its position in the retail sector. This has resulted in EU-compliant services standards for over three years and allowed the Hungarian state to close the financial services negotiations with the EU.

9.6 Concluding thoughts and future research

Concluding a conceptual and empirical study of this nature poses many challenges for the authors. First, there is an inherent temptation to attempt to make bold claims on the basis of the research carried out. The essential dilemma resides in whether the limited empirical research could justify such a bold claim. Second, the research itself has certain shortcomings and if it could have been carried out again these could have been addressed. Certainly, informational constraints as well as the usual time and resource constraints associated with academic research 'informed' the research outcomes in our study. Third, how can the research carried out aid future research and further push empirical and conceptual boundaries? This is perhaps the easiest challenge as there are always areas for further research to augment our limited work. It is these three challenges that the last section of our study will address.

9.6.1 Can our research be generalized?

In writing this study, we have attempted to pose conceptual questions about the relationship between regulatory convergence in the world political economy and the role played by the MNE in this process. Rather than focusing on the conceptually and empirically well-established work exploring the direct political influence of the MNE in the world political economy, we chose to examine an area somewhat less researched: how MNE strategy and especially the pursuit of competitive advantage indirectly promotes or hinders regulatory convergence.

We chose the case of EU enlargement for two reasons. First, EU enlargement is probably the greatest process of regulatory convergence in the world political economy to date and thus it provides an excellent empirical 'test' of our conceptual claims. Second, the role of MNEs in the economic and political structures of the EU and ECE is significant and, as noted above, the political and economic impact of the MNE on Europe has been well documented. Thus on both conceptual and empirical levels, EU enlargement was an excellent case.

Hungary was chosen as our country case study as the role of MNEs in the economic and political life of Hungary is probably more pervasive than in the EU in general, with foreign ownership of industry accounting for as much as half of Hungarian annual GDP.

Our initial conceptual central claim was that as the participation of MNEs in a given sector increased, the ability with which a government could achieve regulatory convergence towards higher international standards would improve. This was because the competitive 'rules of the game' in a given sector would be set by the higher standards used by MNEs as their tool of competitive advantage against local rivals. This competitive process would 'force' local companies to raise standards and, thus, when the issue of introducing new legislation based on these higher standards was tackled by national legislators, the political pressure from domestic industrial interests to resist the new laws would be reduced. This 'internationalization' of domestic regulatory issues was central to our understanding of regulatory convergence.

As part of the methodology used in our study, we chose to focus on market-serving FDI in three sectors: banking, telecommunications and electricity. We believed *a priori* that these sectors would enable us to illustrate the role played by MNEs in their exploitation of competitive regulatory advantage.

As our research proceeded, an important, and with hindsight, obvious modification to this conceptual claim was that MNEs investing in market-serving FDI were more likely to make use of higher standards where competitive pressures required them to do so. Thus, our second claim was that the higher the actual or potential competitive threat posed to MNEs in market-serving FDI, the more likely that higher standards will be used to compete with local rivals.

Given these two claims we found that regulatory convergence, *ceteris paribus*, was promoted more vigorously in the banking sector in Hungary than in telecommunications and electricity because actual competition from fellow MNEs and a well-established local rival, OTP Bank, forced them to leverage their competitive regulatory advantage. In the telecommunications sector, and to a lesser degree in the electricity sector, the realization among MNEs that potential competition from future liberalization required them to be prepared for the onset of actual competition contributed to the implementation of EU-compliant legislation, although at a much slower pace than in banking.

The structural nature of the electricity and telecommunications sectors, both being network industries in which investment in networks represents a substantial element of total investment, meant that regulators in Hungary needed to strike the correct balance between encouraging MNEs to invest in new infrastructure and in promoting competition. Clearly these two aims run counter to each other in the short term and thus regulators were conscious of this in granting temporary exclusivity to the MNEs who had acquired ownership in the sectors.

On the basis of these findings, what can we generalize about the Hungarian experience that we have examined? First, the role of the MNE in exploiting higher standards as part of its pursuit of competitive advantage can have a profound impact on national regulatory structures and in the convergence of differing national systems of regulation. This is especially the case where states are seeking to align national regulations with international agreements or standards. As the world political economy experiences increasing 'system friction' as differing systems of national regulation come into conflict, one finding from our study that could inform this issue is that MNEs can act as pervasive 'transmitters' or 'convergers' of regulatory systems. Rather than pursuing explicit and direct political lobbying, they do so by exerting an influence on the 'rules of entry' by setting standards in the industry. While we do not claim that MNEs drive standards towards global standards as our literature review in Chapter 3 demonstrated, MNE strategies are considerably more complex and they can have a significant impact on a regional level.

Could our analysis be extended to other regions of the world economy such as NAFTA, Latin America and Asia? While the degree of regulatory agreements between states in these other regions is not as extensive as in the EU, it may be interesting to examine similar processes elsewhere.

Another important aspect of our findings, but not necessarily of direct relevance to our research, is the role played by the MNE in the economic development of the transition economy. In all three cases we examined, FDI had a profound and largely positive impact on the development of infrastructure and the development of market institutions. By providing the necessary capital investment and managerial expertise in the sectors we examined, the MNE has transformed the sectors in which they invested, probably bringing change to the sector at a pace that could not have been achieved if alternative means of privatization such as voucher schemes or sales to existing national managements had been adopted.

In this sense, our study provides a useful empirical contribution to the understanding of transition economies and the role played by MNEs in the development of these political economies. Similar studies could be carried out for other ECE political economies using a similar approach to the one we use here.

Thus, we argue that within limits our research is both applicable to other ECE and European cases as well as being a crucial, more general application of the role of the MNE in regulatory convergence and its role in economic development in transition and developing economies.

9.6.2 What are the shortcomings and limits to our research?

We are at pains to stress that our research is not universally applicable. In section 9.4, dealing with policy-making implications, we were keen to stress that our findings were made under a series of assumptions. Thus, for example, should we seek to examine resource-seeking FDI, the regulatory convergence narrative that we considered in our study would only hold if the final destination of production was to the EU from Hungary. If the MNE was using Hungary as a production base for other markets outside the EU, there is no guarantee that they will impose EU product standards for sale elsewhere in the region.

Second, we considered only three cases in Hungary. This means that not all sectors will replicate the experience of those that we considered. For example, the agricultural sector is unlikely to be reformed in the way in which industrial sectors have been affected. We could also consider sectors in which the *acquis* does not have a fully liberalized and EU-level regulated role such as media and transport. In both these cases, despite the presence of MNEs in Hungary, we would not expect to see similar processes of regulatory convergence at work.

Third, we considered only one country. We may have had different results in other political economies in the ECE region. It is hard to make sensible *a priori* claims about what we would expect but, for example, would there have been a different set of outcomes if we had examined an ECE political economy that had a lower level of FDI such as Slovenia?

Fourth, and most importantly, we are by no means claiming that FDI is a universal remedy for dilemmas of economic development for transition and developing economies. Principally, Hungary is in a fortunate position by virtue of the fact that it is geo-politically and geo-economically well-located. On a political level, EU member states are committed to Hungarian inclusion into the EU, regarding it as a compatible state, political economy and society among current member states. Its shared border with Austria makes it an attractive location for MNEs. We can thus contrast Hungary's position with that of the Ukraine that has not even been invited to negotiate membership of the EU. A similar argument can be given for the Russian Federation which in terms of market size is huge but whose political and economic situation is so unstable that EU membership would appear to be impossible for the foreseeable future.

This argument could be extended to refute a more general claim about the role of FDI in developing political economies in general. Structural factors militate against the participation of a range of developing economies in Sub-Saharan Africa and thus no degree of liberal FDI policy could aid the development of these political economies since the attractiveness of these locations for FDI are low as market-serving and resource-seeking criteria. An absence of functioning and stable political institutions in many developing political economies means that despite their attractiveness in terms of resources or even market growth potential, it is unlikely that the MNE is the solution to the challenge of development.

9.6.3 Implications and suggestions for future research

Having outlined possible applications of our work and examined its shortcomings, the last section of this chapter considers the implications of our study for future research. On a conceptual level, we believe that our findings have contributed to a synthesis of the IB and IPE literatures by examining how competitive advantage and strategy can impact on political, legislative and regulatory change. By focusing on the indirect political effect of competitive advantage, our aim has been to build a dialogue between scholars of IPE and IB by bringing politics and strategy closer together intellectually. In this sense, further analyses of the relationship between regulatory convergence and competitive advantage would be an important contribution to this emerging synthesis.

As for the well-established body of literature concerned with European integration, we believe that our study has made an important contribution to our understanding of the current process of EU enlargement on both a conceptual and empirical level. On a conceptual level, we have offered a novel conceptual link between regulatory convergence, a central issue in EU studies research, and the role played by competitive advantage in this process. To date, regulatory convergence has been examined by political scientists in terms of political institutions and the role played by advocacy and lobby groups; by economists in terms of the most efficient regulatory regimes; and by public administration scholars in terms of necessary administrative and bureaucratic changes.

On an empirical level, we have examined Hungary and thus have contributed to the literature on Hungary's accession to the EU. We have also taken three key sectors in Hungary and, to date, we are not aware of other scholars who have adopted our approach to these sectors.

Lastly, we believe that we have contributed to an ongoing debate about the role played by the MNE in the economic development of transition economies and in the process of political change. By providing much-needed capital for infrastructural development and through introducing Western management techniques, the role of MNEs has been crucial in increasing the competitiveness and efficiency of Hungarian-based companies.

We have suggested that the political resistance to change in transition economies is reduced by the role of MNEs upgrading industry standards and thereby lowering adjustment costs when a state attempts to raise national standards to align them with international standards. This facilitates legislative change as elected politicians are under less pressure to slow down new legislation in order to protect the interests of domestic capitalists and workers.

Thus given these contributions to the range of fields discussed above, we tentatively suggest the following areas for future research.

First, it would be interesting to consider the role of resource-seeking FDI and regulatory convergence. What is the impact of regulatory competitive advantage in sectors dominated by resource-seeking FDI?

Second, we believe that important empirical research could be done in other ECE political economies and without doubt this would add to the comparative perspective. If similar patterns emerge in other ECE political economies, and there is a link to the role of FDI, it will enable researchers to build up a more comprehensive picture across the entire region.

Third, this approach could be applied to other regions in the world economy – especially as WTO rules begin to extend beyond the border measures and issues of national regulation come under the scrutiny of convergence and harmonization.

Notes

1. Introduction

1 These are the Czech Republic, Bulgaria, Estonia, Latvia, Lithuania, Romania, Hungary, Poland, Slovakia, Malta, Cyprus and Slovenia. Turkey is included but as a separate issue from this book.

2 Inevitably, this book will generate debate within the discipline. It does not seek to deny the role of other explanations for the phenomena discussed in this work.

3 By democratic or accountable, we mean that during the post-World War Two era in which Keynesian full employment was the primary goal of macroeconomic policy-making, governments pursued economic policies that sought to achieve explicit social objectives. This implies that job creation and explicit redistribution of wealth through a progressive system of taxation was a focus of governmental concern. In principle, failure by elected governments to achieve these objectives meant that the electorate could replace these governments through a democratic pluralist party system. Firms, by contrast, are required to respond to narrower shareholder or ownership objectives related to some measure of profitability or revenue maximization. Often, it is the case that shareholder value tends to ignore broader social concerns, e.g. impact on employment, the environment and social infrastructure. Moreover, firms will tend to focus on short-term maximization targets for fear of the value of their share equity falling. In this sense, wealth creation by the MNE is less democratic.

2. Setting the Scene

1 There are important, and a growing number of, exceptions to this. Stopford and Strange (1991) is a seminal work on the bargaining relationship between the state and the MNE. Cutler et al. (1999) is a broad-based exploration of the role of 'private authority'.

2 In addition, an increasing number of economists, disenchanted by the perceived irrelevance of the theoretical aspects of the subject, have developed into business scholars too.

3 There are few centres for the study of the politics within business schools. Thunderbird Graduate School of International Management has a department of international studies. Georgetown University brings faculty from the McDonough Business School and the School of Foreign Service together in the Landegger Center for Business Diplomacy. The Kennedy School's Center for Business and Government at Harvard University is another example of IPE–IBS collaboration. In the UK, Reading University's

Economics Department has several scholars studying MNE–state relations, including John Dunning.

4 This is related to a contentious debate between economics and IBS about the causes of international trade and investment. Traditionally, economic analysis focused on why countries traded. There was no examination of the firm-based motives for trade as one of the key assumptions of Ricardian and Hecksher-Ohlinian theories was the international immobility of factors of production. When confronted with the empirical reality that MNEs exist, traditional trade theorists would argue that exchange rate movements and trade barriers explained international production. IBS scholars have, almost by definition, been interested in the motives of firms producing internationally and therefore the macroeconomic explanations, while providing a useful structural background to a theory, are unsatisfactory when we are seeking to explain firm-based motives for international production.

5 Actually, the work of Charles Kindleberger (in Buckley 1992) argued that the MNE was a result of imperfectly competitive markets where competition was based on differentiated products. In fact, he argued that rather than being a force for undermining competition, the MNE improved efficiency by breaking up domestic monopolies and surmounting government barriers to trade (Buckley 1992: 6).

6 Examples to illustrate this would be the recent conflict between British car workers and the German management of Rover.

7 This was arguably the difference between the positions taken by the EU Commission and the US Department of Justice in the blocking of the GE–Honeywell merger. The European authorities took a final product market view of the merger, arguing that the new entity could potentially force out rivals from the jet engine market and refused to authorize the merger. Their US counterparts agreed to the merger, basing their reasoning largely on an efficiency of transaction cost approach. See Akbar (2002) for a discussion of the case.

8 This is common in the steel, car and chemical industries where, faced with increased competition, firms may engage in a price war – to the detriment of all firms in the sector. This has also led to the creation of legislation in the EU and in Japan of the 'crisis cartel' that permits price maintenance in the face of falling demand.

9 This was described by a senior manager at British Steel as 'putting a tank on your opponent's lawn': an insurance against a threat from a rival.

10 Thus, the fact that a firm may carry out different aspects of its research in different parts of the world is a testament to the local knowledge base.

11 Primary activities are the main activity of the firm such as production of goods and services. Support activities are those activities that ensure that the primary ones are carried out, e.g. finance and marketing.

12 This is largely because the theoretical and empirical focus of the book refers to the process of regulatory convergence between industrialized political economies.

13 See Rosamond (2000) for a detailed discussion of this debate.

14 The Single European Act created a legal framework for the completion of the common market in the EU.

15 UNICE is the Union of Industrial and Employers Confederations of Europe.

16 UNICE Press Release, 'UNICE calls for alternatives to regulation', Brussels, 29 November 2000.

17 The debate on globalization and shifting power relations between the public and private is well documented. See Palan and Abbot (1998); Browne and Akbar (2001) for a discussion of these issues.

18 Arguably, Cawson's research on HDTV demonstrates this kind of techno-logically 'regressive' influence the CLO and/or MNE may have on policy-makers. It has become clear that digital TV should have (and was) implemented through normal TVs rather than the costly HDTV models that European producers were seeking to develop and encouraging EU policy-makers to adopt.

19 Technocratic policy-making inevitably requires the setting up of agencies that are subject to regulatory capture. However, there should be no reason to suggest that this may be different at an IO level when compared to a national/domestic level.

20 The BIS's work is informed directly by commercial banking practices.

21 The traditional view is that few firms themselves directly lobby – rather they make use of industry-wide trade associations.

22 This is a clear (rhetorical) demonstration of MNEs' structural power in the GPE – an issue that we shall return to in more detail below.

23 These forms are numerous, ranging from bilateral tax treaties to multilateral regimes on the provision of services. In between, there have been notable regional integration projects such as the EU, the North American Free Trade Agreement (NAFTA) and its South American counterpart (Mercosur).

24 An interesting outcome of the internationalization of economic policy-making has been the emergence of a common political agenda between nationalist political groups and traditional socialist groups who both fear the loss of sovereignty that this process implies. Furthermore, direct action at headline international meetings has developed a broad mix of civil society protest against 'globalization' and the allegedly collu-sive role governments play in forwarding MNE commercial interests.

25 There are fewer better examples of the pervading role for public regulation than the EU Commission's rejection of the world's largest industrial merger between GE and Honeywell.

26 It is interesting to note that the world's best-selling English language text on international business by Daniels and Radebaugh (2001) incorporates specific chapters on the political role of the MNE and each chapter has an 'ethical dilemma case study'.

27 The theme of the 2001 US Academy of Management Annual Convention was concerned with 'Why Governments Matter'.

28 The New Academy of Business offers a joint MSc with the University of Bath in the UK on Responsible Management. A consortium of international universities including INSEAD (France), McGill University (Canada) and Lancaster University (UK) have an MBA for Practising Managers devoted

to engendering an ethical dimension to decision-making in business. Lastly, Lancaster University offers a doctoral and research master's programme in 'Critical Management'. London Business School's 'Regulation Initiative' is also a leading research programme into the relationship between business and governmental regulation.

3. Regulatory Convergence

1 It is of course important to recognize that this chapter focuses on the *transnational* focus of political activity of firms. Political science theory based on domestic politics has long understood the salience of the firm as a political actor.

2 The debate over the efficiency of the state is a long and complex one and certainly one that is beyond the scope of this chapter. It is generally argued in the neo-classical, public choice literature that states become captured by vested interests. Rather than responding to the overall welfare of society, states tend to respond to those groups most able to mobilize political resources in their favour.

3 Thus, a core competence in distribution and sales granted Honda motorcycles an advantage over its US rivals in the 1970s and 1980s.

4 Arguably, the EU's Block Exemption on automobile sales is an example of firms guaranteeing their core competence. Alternatively, the Block Exemption has come under criticism for allowing car firms to maintain price segmentation in the EU car market.

5 Again, it is possible to consider the role of ISO standards. Firms aim to secure their competitive advantage through ISO standards and these are commonly based on a core competence of firms in the sector concerned.

6 This does not imply that harmonization to one standard or set of regulations emerges. Rather, states develop mechanisms, e.g. mutual recognition of national standards.

7 An example of this is the case of VHS as a video standard or Microsoft Windows OS for PC.

8 They could, of course, develop their own technology to compete.

9 An illustration of this has been the way in which firms in countries seeking to join the European Union have been exhorted by governments to prepare ahead of membership.

10 A similar argument is forwarded where trade liberalization leads to an increase in intra- rather than inter-industry trade. This is because the relocation of factors of production *within* industries is less costly and drawn out than relocation *between* industries.

11 In the social sphere such as labour market regulation, this is sometimes referred to as 'social dumping'.

12 Again in the social and environmental spheres this is especially relevant.

13 MNEs that invest in large developing markets such as India may well produce products to lower standards in order to compete with local companies who produce 'clone' versions of the MNE's product.

14 Both at a regional and multilateral level, states have begun to develop agreements on common standards and mutual recognition in order to overcome the danger that national standards become non-tariff barriers.

15 These rules could, for example, concern the use of child labour, use of environmentally harmful sub-products etc.

16 Some of these are discussed in part one above.

17 This is unless the service can somehow be traded internationally and the MNE motivation is to exploit lower factor cost for export.

18 This is not an unrealistic assumption as the growth of regional and multi-lateral accords has been a feature of the last few decades in the GPE.

19 To this extent, this chapter disassociates itself from the prescriptive work of economists such as the 'Shock Therapists', e.g. Jeffrey Sachs, who has argued that liberalization of the domestic economy is part of a one-stop cure for transition and developing economies. Indeed, in the face of the reality of some of the outcomes of Sach's prescriptions, he has retracted some of his claims.

4. The Empirical Setting

1 We are not suggesting that this process is inevitable or irreversible. It is still possible for leading industrialized states to limit the degree of inter-national economic integration. Nor are we suggesting that this process is unambiguously beneficial to all groups in society. We are merely observing that this process has occurred and appears to be intensifying.

2 This implies that while the enlargements of 1974 (UK, Ireland and Denmark), 1981 (Greece), 1986 (Spain and Portugal) and 1995 (Sweden, Finland and Austria) were significant projects for the national administrations of these countries, the current round of enlargement, coming more than four decades after the EU's creation, and involving former communist states, is likely to be the most difficult.

3 That is not to suggest that countries with low levels of FDI have been unsuccessful. The success of economic transition cannot be located in one or two variables.

4 See Moravscik (1998), Richardson (1996), Rosamond (2000), Wallace and Wallace (2000) for detailed and competing explanations for EU integration and policy-making.

5 Legal scholars of EU integration examine three kinds of legal instruments. First, there is an EU regulation. This is the most stringent of EU rules. A regulation must be implemented in all member states, be applicable to all legal personalities and must be transferred into national law in the exact wording of the regulation. The second instrument is the directive. While, like a regulation, it must be implemented and be applicable in all mem-ber states and on all legal personalities, it can be transferred into national law in the most efficient way according to national legal systems. The third instrument is the recommendation. As the name suggests, it is not legally binding and acts only as a guide to member states.

6 There are numerous studies on the political economy of EU integration. One of the most comprehensive and accessible is Tsoukalis (1997). More recent studies include El-Agraa (2001).

7 An excellent example of this was related to the deregulation of capital markets and the banking sector. The EU created a Single Banking Licence based on the Second Banking Directive in order to facilitate cross-border banking services.

8 This referred to a freedom of movement of goods, services, capital and people.

9 Jacques Delors asked Lord Cockfield, UK Commissioner and an appointee of the UK Prime Minister, Margaret Thatcher, to write this chapter and to push member states to implement its recommendations.

10 One of the great ironies of the Thatcher premiership was that, as the most outspoken critic of European deepening integration, by signing the SEA the UK Prime Minister facilitated the creation of the EMU!

11 Of course, there was a strong element of rhetoric involved in this proclamation. There remained significant areas such as Air Transport, Energy and Public Procurement in which EU legislation had not been fully implemented in all member states or had not even been agreed by member states in the Council of Ministers. Nevertheless, the fact that a majority of the new legislation had been agreed and implemented was a remarkable political feat.

12 Even the most Europhile of analysts have been amazed at the success of EU integration in the 1990s.

13 Indeed, numerous interviews for research into a range of policy areas illustrated the mindset of the technocratic policy-maker. The overwhelming attitude was to ensure that ill-informed ministers would not have to agree final details as this could hold up the process. Thus, as many decisions as possible were taken before details arrived at the ministerial council.

14 This is a clear (rhetorical) demonstration of MNEs' structural power in the GPE – an issue that we shall return to in more detail below.

15 In the early 1990s, EFTA consisted of Sweden, Norway, Austria, Switzerland, Liechtenstein, Iceland and Finland. Switzerland and Liechtenstein rejected EEA membership in a referendum.

16 The EFTA Surveillance Authority was set up to advise EFTA member states on developments in the Single Market. It could produce reports, sometimes critical of the EU, but had no legislative role.

17 The rump EFTA member states Iceland, Switzerland and Liechtenstein now appear to have abandoned attempts to join the EU for the foreseeable future.

18 It is important to note that competition policy for several member states is a relatively new concept. Among the current member states, the UK and Germany have the longest-standing national anti-trust authorities.

19 Readers are encouraged to follow up references cited in the following section for a detailed analysis of the process of economic and political transition.

20 Unsurprisingly, this led some US commentators, notably Francis Fukuyama, to claim that the contest for ideas was over – all democratic societies

eventually become liberal democracies based on free markets and minimal government intervention.

21 This is somewhat at odds with the early literature (e.g. IMF 1993; Gros and Steinherr 1995) that set up a dichotomy between political economies that pursued a gradualist reform process and those who pursued a 'Shock Therapy' solution to the challenges of transition.

22 A notable exception to this has been the case of Belarus which, under the autocratic leadership of Lukashenko, has undertaken virtually no reforms and is currently seeking reintegration with Russia.

23 See Zaszlavsky (1994) for an illuminating discussion on the microeconomic problems of socialist political economies.

24 Numerous examples of industrial espionage by ECE states as they attempted to garner military and industrial technology are witness to this chronic shortage of technological infrastructure.

25 This was a consequence of Janos Kadar, Hungarian Socialist Party leader, who, in the light of the 1956 revolution against the socialists, combined the threat of military control from the Soviet Union with a political *laissez-faire* attitude towards limited private enterprise to control Hungarian society.

26 Again, the leaders of the socialist parties in both Romania (Ceaucescu) and Albania (Enver Hoxha) sought to distance themselves from the Soviet Union. Unlike the Yugoslav state, they were less liberal in their foreign policies towards West Europe.

27 Czechoslovakia, in 1968, attempted a similar revolution to the Hungarians but this too was ruthlessly crushed by Soviet military operations.

28 This section does not aim to offer an exhaustive account of the institutional changes after 1989. The reader is recommended to follow up the references in the text.

29 At a seminar held at Sussex University's European Institute in 1994, Leszek Balcerowicz, the then Finance Minister of Poland, responding to a question about the role of welfare states in transitional Poland, stated simply that the Polish had no money for a welfare state.

30 By foreign capital, we are not referring to portfolio flows of capital from abroad. We are interested in capital for productive purposes, i.e. FDI.

31 There are several kinds of privatization programmes that were adopted by ECE governments: these included domestic voucher programmes as used in the Czech Republic and Russia, transfer of ownership to existing management under market conditions (sometimes called 'Spontaneous Privatization' as this occurred without the permission of the state) and sales to foreign owners.

32 This problem was further worsened by the reality that some people, living in such a desperate situation, would sell their shares immediately in order to acquire some money to buy basic living requirements.

33 'Cherry picking' is where a business seeks to acquire only the most valuable of assets in an acquisition. In the context of enterprise privatization, this meant that foreign companies would buy only enterprises that had a realistic market value while asset stripping others to gain the little market value that was there.

34 This was largely the case in Hungary where whole companies were sold to foreigners setting in train the process of MNE activity that is the subject of our book.

35 Indeed, one of the most challenging aspects about writing about the ECE transition process is that the specificities of each experience make it difficult to draw general, and useful, conclusions.

36 These include most of the candidate countries from the region.

37 The degree to which the EU is actually prepared to bar membership on the basis of the political criteria is debatable but is unfortunately outside the scope of our discussion.

38 Again, we can find exceptions to this claim. For example, the Estonian government argued that the current EU rules were less liberal than their own and that, consequently, EU membership threatened the highly liberal nature of Estonia's political economy.

39 Interview with Thomas McClenaghan, DG Enterprise, EU Commission.

40 A confidential working document produced for DG Enlargement in July 2000 made clear that candidate countries could not join by simply demonstrating amended statutes – it would be incumbent on them to provide administrative resources to back this up.

41 Meskó, A. (2001), 'A Külföldi töke szerepe Magyarországon' (The Role of Foreign Capital in Hungary), *Gazdaság és Statisztika*, 2001/14, p. 1.

42 Ibid.

43 EBRD Investment Profile 2001, Hungary, p. 9.

44 EBRD Investment Profile 2001, Hungary, p. 7.

45 Ibid.

46 Ibid.

47 Endre Juhasz, Hungarian Ambassador to the EU, during comments over EU accession negotiations, claimed that while the current tax incentives would contravene EU rules, it is likely that the Hungarian state will reorient the regime to target regional development objectives rather than a blanket exemption as it currently stands.

5. Case Study Methodology

1 This of course is a static argument. MNE strategy in developing countries could also be based on first mover advantage in a growing market of soon to be wealthy consumers. In an interview with a senior manager at Unilever for other research in June 1999, it was suggested that developing countries offer opportunities for MNEs to sell 'outdated' products as a means of capturing market share which allows them eventually to offer leading brands as the countries become wealthier.

2 Interviews with production managers at GE Lighting, Budapest, Hungary, July 2000.

3 This would also be encouraged by a desire to meet economies of scale across a larger market. For marketing purposes, this requires multilingual packaging and distribution channels.

4 It is likely that the Hungarian Parliament will cede legislative control to the regulatory bodies granting them full independence from the government.
5 Interview with Peter Bakos-Blumentahl, General Manager, CIB Bank Hungary.

6. Banking and Financial Services

1 Views of a senior Postabank manager, February 2001.
2 Interviews with Tamas Simonyi, Managing Director of Rabobank Hungaria Kft and with Istvan Preda, Company Secretary, ABN-AMRO Bank Kft. Rabobank is a Dutch bank that deals with Dutch companies in Hungary in the agro-alimentary sector.
3 This was very unlike countries such as Mexico, where a powerful domestic class of extremely wealthy investors was available to quickly repurchase the banks that had been nationalized by the government some ten years before.
4 Similar effects have also been noted in regions within nations, such as the American south, a historically capital-poor region, where inter-state banking brought a much wider availability of funds to finance business growth and consumer spending in states such as South Carolina.
5 Gyorgy Szekeley, retired Senior Banker at Banca Commerciale Italiana, claimed in one of our interviews that foreign ownership was central to the improvement of balance sheets and lending practices.
6 Interview with Peter Bakos-Blumenthal, General Manager, CIB Bank Ltd.
7 Interview with Akos Dolle, Treasury, Postabank.
8 Such as Slovakia, Romania, Ukraine or Yugoslavia and with the exception of Slovenia.
9 See De Soto (2000) for a treatment of the subject of why financial markets in developing countries remain weak.
10 Interview with Tamas Simonyi, CEO Rabobank Hungary and Peter Bakos Blumenthal, General Manager CIB-Bank Ltd.
11 Bakos-Blumenthal, General Manager CIB-Bank Ltd.
12 Confidential interview with a senior manager of one of Hungary's top five banks.
13 'EU Conformity Around Corner for Hungarian Bank Regulators', Huntrade Press Release, London, January 2000.
14 See Dixon (1992) for a full discussion of these issues.
15 Until the creation of the ECB and the Euro, monetary policy considerations and bank operations were maintained under the host-country principle.
16 See Tsoukalis (1997) and El-Agraa (2001) for discussions of the impact on market structure of the Second Banking Directive.
17 Comment made by Endre Juhasz, Head of Hungarian Delegation to the EU.
18 Op. cit. #13.
19 Ibid.
20 Of course, this result may not hold for resource-seeking FDI where MNEs are motivated to enter a foreign political economy in order to access

low-cost resources. Here competition induced by FDI does not necessarily have the effect of upgrading industry standards. If anything, it may maintain industrial standards at the lower level, as that is the cost-efficiency of operating there, or even reduce them further as local companies have to lower their standards to compete.

7. The Electricity Sector

1   Interview with Pal Ligeti, Ministry of Economics, 20 August 2001.
2   The experience of UK railway privatization is an instructive illustration of the problems of encouraging investment without restricting competition.
3   Interview with the Director of the Hungarian Energy Office, Dr Peter Kaderjak, 19 August 2001.
4   Interview with Allan Walmsley, General Manager, Csepeli Áramtermelö Rt.
5   Magyar Energia Hivatal (2000), 'Report on the Activities of the Hungarian Energy Office in 2000', Budapest, December 2000, p. 30.
6   Interviews with confidential industry sources and the Director of the Hungarian Energy Office, Dr Peter Kaderjak.
7   Interview with Pal Ligeti.
8   Directive 96/92/EC of the European Parliament and of the Council of 19 December 1996 concerning common rules for the internal market in electricity.
9   Report on the Electricity Sector by the Hungarian Energy Office: http://www.eh.gov.hu/angol/indexf_a.htm.
10 Confidential industry sources and interviews with Peter Kaderjak, Director of the Hungarian Energy Office and with Pal Ligeti, Head of Energy Policy at the Ministry of Economics.
11 Interview with Peter Kaderjak.
12 Parallels can be drawn with the experience of the UK rail privatization where a lack of genuine competition between train operating companies combined with long franchises did not encourage fixed capital upgrading.
13 Confidential industry interviews and views of Ligeti and Kaderjak.
14 Ibid.
15 Op. cit. #93, p. 17.
16 Peter Kaderjak pointed out that the Hungarian model was based on a British approach towards privatization.
17 Interview with Borbala Toth, coordinator, International Affairs, Hungarian Energy Office.
18 Interview with Pal Ligeti.
19 Ibid.
20 'Negotiating Position of the Government of the Republic of Hungary on Chapter 14 – Energy', CONF-H 26/99, Brussels, 18 May 1999.
21 Hungarian Energy Office, Annual Report of Activities, 2001.
22 'MVM Rt Liberalization Press Release', March 2001.
23 Views of confidential industry sources.
24 Ibid.

25 Interview with Allan Walmsley, General Manager, Csepeli Áramtermelö Rt.
26 At the Csepeli 2 plant, GE provided the electricity turbine and the physical structure was provided by a range of German companies.
27 Op. cit. #139.
28 Ibid. At the Csepel plant for example, the total employment went from 1700 workers to as few as 80. This was primarily related to the fact that the number of activities that the plant was performing was substantially reduced.

8. Telecommunications

1 Interview with Luise Pape Moller, Telecommunications Researcher, Department of Political Science, Aarhus University.
2 Hungarian Communication Authority (2000), 'Hungarian Telecommunications Regulatory Environment and Authority', p. 5.
3 'Reform and Development of the Hungarian Telecommunications', presentation by Professor Gyula Sallai, Executive Vice President, Communication Authority, 28 April 1999, Budapest.
4 Hungarian Communication Authority (2000), 'Telecommunications in Hungary at the Millennium', p. 6.
5 Ibid.
6 Ibid.
7 Op. cit. #93, p. 12.
8 Ibid., p. 8.
9 Ibid., p. 9.
10 Ibid., p.18.
11 Telenor recently acquired 100 per cent of Pannon shares when KPN Telecom sold its remaining shares.
12 There is a fourth mobile telephone company called Westel 450 which operates on an analogue frequency but it has a declining number of subscribers, and in 2000 possessed around only 3 per cent of the total market.
13 Op. cit. #9, p. 20.
14 Ibid., p. 22.
15 Ibid., p. 27.
16 Op. cit. #93, p. 13.
17 Ibid., p. 33.
18 Op. cit. #2, p. 5.
19 See Hungarian Communication Authority (2000), 'Hungarian Telecommunications Regulatory Environment and Authority', for a detailed discussion and listing of these legal instruments.
20 Ibid., pp. 22-3.
21 'Research and New Technologies: Applicant Countries and the Community *acquis*: Hungary', December 2001, EU Commission Report, Brussels.
22 Commission Report COM (2000) 705 final.
23 Interview with Cecilia Marta, Legal Counsel, MATÁV.

24 Ibid.
25 Interview with Peter Fath, Executive Director, AmCham Hungary.
26 Interview with Gabor Szekeres, CFO and Deputy CEO, Axelero.
27 Interview by Luise Pape Moller with Tibor Soos, telecommunications lawyer.
28 Hungarian Communication Authority (2001), 'Ownership Structure of the Hungarian Telecommunications Market', p. 5.
29 Ibid.
30 Ibid., p. 7.
31 Ibid., p. 8.
32 Ibid.
33 See Hungarian Communication Authority (2001), 'Ownership Structure of the Hungarian Telecommunications Market' for a detailed discussion of these companies and their presence in the Hungarian telecommunications sector.
34 Siemens Kft company figures.
35 Op. cit. #28, p. 19.
36 Ibid.
37 The 3.5 GHz bandwidth is important because it allows for both data communication and voice communication services. In particular, it will allow telecommunications services companies to access end-users without the need to make use of the infrastructure of the LTOs.
38 Op. cit. #31, p. 26.
39 Confidential interview with telecoms industry consultant.
40 Ibid.
41 As noted by the EU Commission in its last report on progress towards implementation of the *acquis*, the Commission stated in respect of the Czech telecommunications sector: 'The date of 1 January 2001 for full liberalisation was fixed in 1994, but the provision of carrier selection facilities that are vital to effective competition has been unjustifiably delayed. This has undermined the market opening and has hindered new entrants in certain respects. This is harmful to the interests of consumers and of investors in companies which compete with the incumbent operator in which the state has a financial interest. This situation should be rectified without further delay.'

9. Conclusions

1 Comments of Professor Bruno Dallago, University of Trento at an IMC seminar dealing with MNEs and economic transition, June 2001.
2 Interview with Tamas Simonyi, CEO Rabobank Rt.
3 Interview with Peter Bakos-Blumenthal, General Manager, CIB Bank Ltd.
4 Confidential interview with a senior Postabank manager.
5 Interviews with Istvan Preda, Company Secretary, ABN-AMRO Bank Hungary Ltd and Tamas Simonyi, Rabobank Rt.

6 Thus, Rabobank, the Dutch agro-alimentary specialist, serves predominantly Dutch companies involved in the food sector in Hungary.

7 The experience of BT in the UK illustrates the role of competition in eroding a dominant position of a former monopoly. With telecommunications liberalization, BT's market share of fixed-line telephony collapsed to less than 50 per cent from an initial position of over 85 per cent.

8 Among a number of reasons for the appalling results of UK rail privatization is that the UK government's under-investing prior to privatization and then creating regional service monopolies has meant that none of the regional train companies has an incentive to upgrade the service in terms of costly investment in capital machinery.

References

Abel, Istvan, Pierre L. Siklos and Istvan P. Szekely (1998), *Money and Finance in Transforming to a Market Economy* (Cheltenham: Edward Elgar).

Akbar, Y. (2000), 'The International Organization and Private Sector Advocacy: the EU and ACEA'. Unpublished manuscript.

Akbar, Y. (2001), 'Explaining EU–US Commercial Relations: Societal Influences and Trade Disputes'. Unpublished manuscript.

Akbar, Y. (2002), 'Grabbing Victory from the Jaws of Defeat? Can the Failed GE–Honeywell Merger Force International Competition Policy Cooperation?', *World Competition*, 25 (4).

Akbar Y. and J. Brad McBride (2002), 'Multinational Enterprise Strategy, Foreign Direct Investment and Economic Development: the Case of Hungary'. Unpublished manuscript.

Bain, J. (1956), *Barriers to New Competition: Their Character and Consequences in Manufacturing Industries* (Fairfield, NJ: Kelley. Reprint version 1993).

Barnet, R. and John Cavanagh (1994), *Global Dreams: Imperial Corporations and the New World Order* (New York: Simon and Schuster).

Baron, D. (1995), 'Integrated Strategy: Market and Non-Market Components', *California Management Review*, 37 (2): 47–65.

Baron, D. (1997), 'Integrated Strategy, Trade Policy and Global Competition', *California Management Review*, 39 (2): 145–69.

Birkinshaw, Julian and Neil Hood (1998), 'Multinational Subsidiary Evolution: Capability and Charter Change in Foreign-owned Subsidiary Companies', *Academy of Management Review*, 23 (4): 773–95.

Browne, M. J. and Yusaf Akbar (2001), 'Globalization and the Renewal of Social Democracy', in Luke Martell et al., *Social Democracy: National and Global Perspectives* (Basingstoke: Palgrave – now Palgrave Macmillan).

Bruszt, L. and David Stark (1999), *Postsocialist Pathways: Transforming Politics and Property in East Central Europe* (Cambridge: Cambridge University Press).

Buch, C. M. (1997), 'Opening Up for Foreign Banks – Why Central and Eastern Europe Can Benefit', *Economics of Transforming*, (5) 2: 339–66.

Buckley, P. J. (1992), *Studies in International Business* (Basingstoke: Macmillan – now Palgrave Macmillan).

Buckley, P. J. and Mark Casson (1976), *The Future of the Multinational Enterprise* (Basingstoke: Macmillan – now Palgrave Macmillan).

Cantwell, J. (1991), 'A Survey of Theories of International Production', in C. Pitelis and Roger Sugden (eds), *The Nature of the Transnational Firm* (London: Routledge).

Casson, M. (1985), 'Multinational Monopolies and International Cartels', in Peter J. Buckley and Mark Casson, *The Economic Theory of the Multinational Enterprise* (Basingstoke: Macmillan – now Palgrave Macmillan).

Casson, M. (1987), *The Firm and the Market* (Oxford: Basil Blackwell).

Casson, M. (1990), 'International Comparative Advantage and the Location of R&D', *Global Research Strategy and International Competitiveness*, 1990, pp. 68–103.

Caves, R. (1982), *Multinational Enterprises and Economic Analysis* (Cambridge: Cambridge University Press).

Cawson, A. (1995), 'High Definition Television in Europe', *Political Quarterly*, 66/2: 157–73.

Cawson, A. (1997), 'Big Firms as Political Actors: Corporate Power and the Governance of the European Consumer Electronics Industry'. Chapter 9 in Wallace and Young (1997).

Cerny, Philip G. (1995), 'Globalization and the Changing Logic of Collective Action', *International Organization*, 49 (4): 595–625.

Coase, R. (1996), *Environmental Economics and Policy: Selected Classical Readings* (Prague: University of Economics Press).

Coen, D. (1997), 'Evolution of the Large Firm as a Political Actor in the European Union', *Journal of European Public Policy*, 4 (1): 91–108.

Coen, D. and Wyn Grant (2000), 'Corporate Political Strategy and Global Policy: a Case Study of the Transatlantic Business Dialogue', *London Business School Regulation Initiative Discussion Chapter*, No. 42, November.

Cowles, M. Green (1997), 'Organizing Industrial Coalitions: a Challenge for the Future?' Chapter 6 in Wallace and Young (1997).

Cowling, K. and Roger Sugden (1987), *Transnational Monopoly Capitalism* (Brighton: Wheatsheaf).

Cox, R. (1996), *Approaches to World Order* (Cambridge: Cambridge University Press).

Cox, R. (1987), *Production, Power, and World Order: Social Forces in the Making of History* (New York: Columbia University Press).

Cutler, A., Haufler, V. and Tony Porter (eds) (1999), *Private Authority and International Affairs* (New York: SUNY Press).

Daniels, J. and C. Radebaugh (2001), *International Business: Environment and Operations* (New Jersey: Prentice Hall).

De Soto, Hernando (2000), *The Mystery of Capital: Why Capitalism Triumphs in the West and Fails Everywhere Else* (New York: Basic Books).

Dixon, J. (1992), *Banking in Europe* (London: Routledge).

Doremus P., Keller W., Pauly, L. and Simon Reich (1998), *The Myth of the Global Corporation* (New Jersey: Princeton University Press).

Doz, Y. (1986), *Strategic Management in Multinational Enterprises* (Oxford: Pergamon Press).

Dunning, J. (1981), *International Production and the Multinational Enterprise* (London: Allen & Unwin).

Dunning, J. (1988a), 'The Eclectic Paradigm of International Production: an Update and Some Possible Extensions', *Journal of International Business Studies*, 19: 1.

Dunning, J. (1988b), 'The Theory of International Production', *International Trade Journal*, 3.

Dunning, J. (1997) (ed.), *Governments, Globalization and International Business* (Oxford: Oxford University Press).

The Economist (1998), 'Eastern Europe's Banks: Reversal of Fortune', *The Economist*, 10 December.

Eden, L. and Evan Potter (eds) (1993), *Multinationals in the Global Political Economy* (New York: St. Martin's Press – now Palgrave Macmillan).

Edwards, S. and S. van Wijnbergen (1987), 'On the Appropriate Timing and Sequencing of Economic Liberalization in Developing Countries', in M. Connolly and C. Gonzalez (eds), *Economic Reforms and Stabilization in Latin America* (New York: St Martin's Press – now Palgrave Macmillan), pp. 71–91.

El-Agraa, A. M. (2001), *The European Union: Policies and Institutions* (London: Longman).

Estrin, S., Hare, P. and M. Suranyi (1992), 'Banking in Transforming: Development and Current Problems in Hungary', *Centre for Economic Performance Discussion Paper*, 68 (London: London School of Economics and Political Science).

Frieden, J. and David Lake (1987), *International Political Economy: Perspectives on Global Power and Wealth* (New York: Routledge).

Fukuyama, F. (1992), *The End of History and the Last Man* (London: Penguin).

Galbraith, J. K. (1971), *The New Industrial State* (London: Penguin).

Getz, K. (1997), 'Research in Corporate Political Action: Integration and Assessment', *Business and Society*, 36 (1): 32–72.

Gill, S. and David Law (1988), *The Global Political Economy: Perspectives, Problems, and Policies* (New York: Harvester Wheatsheaf).

Gilpin, R. (1975), *US Power and the Multinational Corporation: the Political Economy of Foreign Direct Investment* (New York: Basic Books).

Globerman, S. and D. Shapiro (1999), 'The Impact of Government Policies on Foreign Direct Investment: the Canadian Experience', *Journal of International Business Studies*, 30 (3): 513–32.

Graham, E. (1978), 'Transatlantic Investment by Multinational Firms: a Rivalistic Phenomenon?' *Journal of Post Keynesian Economics*, 1 (1): 82–99.

Graham, E. (1985), *Intra-industry Direct Foreign Investment, Market Structure, Firm Rivalry and Technological Performance* (New York: St. Martin's Press).

Greider, W. (1992), *One World, Ready or Not: the Manic Logic of Global Capitalism* (New York: Simon and Schuster).

Gros, D. and Edward Steinherr (1995), *Winds of Change* (London: Longman).

Haas, E. (1964), *Beyond the Nation State: Functionalism and International Organization* (Stanford: Stanford University Press).

Hix, S. (1999), *The Political System of the European Union* (New York: St. Martin's Press – now Palgrave Macmillan).

Hocking, B. and S. McGuire (2001), 'Towards a Post-Modern Trade Policy? Business Strategies and the Foreign Sales Corporation Issue'. Unpublished manuscript.

Hymer, S. (1968), 'La Grande Firme Multinationale', *Revue Economique*, 19: 949–73.

Jones, D. T., Womack, J. and D. Roos (1990), *The Machine that Changed the World* (Cambridge: MIT Press).

Keohane, R. (1984), *After Hegemony: Co-operation and Discord in the World Political Economy* (Princeton: Princeton University Press).

Keohane, R. and Joseph Nye (1990), *Power and Interdependence* (London: Addison-Wesley-Longman).

Kohler-Koch, B. (1997), 'Organized Interests in European Integration: the Evolution of a New Type of Government?' Chapter 3 in Wallace and Young (1997).

Lawrence, R., Bressand, A. and Ito Takatoshi (1996), *A Vision for the World Economy: Openness, Diversity and Cohesion* (Washington DC: Brookings Institution).

Lawton, T. and S. McGuire (2001), 'Supranational Governance and Firm Strategy: the Emerging Role of the World Trade Organization'. Unpublished manuscript.

Majone, G. (ed.) (1990), *Regulating Europe* (London: Routledge).

Maxwell, J., Rothenberg, S., Briscoe, F. and A. Marcus (1997), 'Green Schemes: Corporate Environmental Strategies and their Implementation', *California Management Review*, 39 (3): 118–34.

Meskó, A. (2001), 'A Külföldi Töke Szerepe Magyarországon', *Gazdaság és Statisztika*, 4: 18–31.

Middlemas, K. (1997), *Orchestrating Europe: the Informal Politics of the European Union 1973–1995* (London: Fontana).

Milner, H. (1988), *Resisting Protectionism* (New York: Columbia University Press).

Milner, H. and David Yoffie (1989), 'Between Free Trade and Protectionism: Strategic Trade Policy and a Theory of Corporate Trade Demands', *International Organization*, 43 (2): 239–72.

Mintzberg, H. (1973), *The Nature of Managerial Work* (New York: Harper and Row).

Moody's (2001), 'Stable Outlook with Selective Upside for Hungarian Banks', *Moody's Investor Services Newswire*, 3 January.

Moran, T. (ed.) (1998), *Managing International Political Risk* (Oxford: Basil Blackwell).

Moravscik, A. (1991), 'Negotiating the Single European Act: National Interests and Conventional Statecraft in the European Community', *International Organization*, 45 (1): 19–56.

Moravscik, A. (1998), *The Choice for Europe: Social Purpose and State Power from Messina to Maastricht* (Ithaca: Cornell University Press).

Murphy, D. (1995), 'Regulation in Open Economies: Competition and Convergence among Jurisdictions', PhD Dissertation, MIT, 1995.

Nelson, R. and Sidney Winter (1977), 'Simulation of Schumpeterian Competition', *American Economic Review*, February 67 (1): 271–6.

Ostry, S. (1990), *Governments and Corporations in a Shrinking World: Trade and Innovation Policies in the United States, Europe and Japan* (New York: Council on Foreign Relations).

Ostry, S. (1994), 'New Dimensions of Market Access: Overview from a Trade Policy Perspective', typescript, OECD Roundtable on the New Dimensions of Market Access in a Globalizing World Economy, 30 June–1 July, Paris.

Palan, R. and John Abbot (1998), *State Strategies in the Global Political Economy* (London: Pinter).

Pavitt, K. (1987), *The Comparative Economics of Research Development and Innovation in East and West: a Survey* (London: Harwood).

Pigman, G. (2001), 'Shap-pei or Wolf in Sheep's Clothing? The World Economic Form from Le Defi Americain to the Bill-Bill Summit'. Unpublished manuscript.

Porter, M. (1980), *Competitive Strategy: Techniques for Analyzing Industries and Competitors* (New York: Free Press).

Porter, M. (1985), *Competitive Advantage: Creating and Sustaining Superior Performance* (New York: Free Press).

Porter, M. (1990), *The Competitive Advantage of Nations* (New York: Free Press).

Prahalad, C. K. and Yves L. Doz (1987), *The Multinational Mission: Balancing Local Demands and Global Vision* (New York: Free Press).

Prahalad, C. K. and Gary Hamel (1990), 'The Core Competence of the Corporation', *Harvard Business Review*, May–June: 78–91.

Prebisch, Raul (1970), *Transformacion y Desarrollo: la Gran Tarea de America Latina* (Mexico City: Fundacion de Cultura Economica).

Richardson, J. (ed.) (1996), *The European Union: Power and Policymaking* (London: Routledge).

Rosamond, B. (2000), *Theories of European Integration* (New York: St. Martin's Press).

Ruggie, J. (1989), *Multilateralism Matters* (New York: Columbia University Press).

Rugman, A. and A. Verbeke (1990), *Global Corporate Strategy and Trade Policy* (London: Routledge).

Rugman, A. and A. Verbeke (1998), 'Multinational Enterprises and Public Policy', *Journal of International Business Studies*, 29 (1): 115–36.

Sachs, J. (1994), *Poland's Jump to the Market Economy* (Cambridge: MIT Press).

Safarian, E. (1993), *Multinational Enterprise and Public Policy: a Study of the Industrial Countries* (Aldershot: Edward Elgar).

Sako, M. (1992), *Prices, Quality and Trust: Inter-firm Relations in Britain and Japan* (Cambridge: Cambridge University Press).

Sallai, G. (1999), 'Reform and Development of the Hungarian Telecommunications', background to presentation, INFO 99, 28 April, Budapest.

Sandholz, W. and John Zysman (1989), 'Recasting the European Bargain', *World Politics*, 42(1): 95–128.

Sanyal, R. and T. Guvenli (2000), 'Relations between Multinational Firms and Host Governments: the Experience of American-Owned Firms in China', *International Business Review*, 9 (2000): 119–34.

Scholte, J. (1996), 'The Geography of Collective Identities in a Globalizing World', *Review of International Political Economy*, 3 (4), Winter.

Scholte, J. (2000), '"In the Foothills": Relations between the IMF and Civil Society', in R. Higgot et al. (eds), *Rethinking Globalizations: from Corporate Transnationalism to Local Interventions* (New York: St. Martin's Press – now Palgrave Macmillan), pp. 13–31.

Sedelemeier, U. and Helen Wallace (2000), 'Policies towards Eastern and Central Europe', in H. Wallace and W. William (eds), *Policymaking in the European Union* (Oxford: Oxford University Press).

Sell, S. (1999), 'Multinational Corporations as Agents of Change: the Globalization of Intellectual Property Rights', Chapter 4 in Cutler et al.

Shaw, M. (1999), *Politics and Globalization: Knowledge, Ethics and Agency* (London: Routledge).

Sinclair, T. (1999), 'Bond Rating Agencies and Coordination in the Global Political Economy'. Chapter 6 in Cutler et al.

Spero, J. (1990), *The Politics of International Economic Relations* (London: Longman).

Stocking, G. W. and Watkins, M. W. (1948), *Cartels or Competition? The Economics of International Controls by Business and Government: With the Report and Recommendations of the Committee on Cartels and Monopoly* (New York: Twentieth Century Fund).

Strange, S. (1986), *Casino Capitalism* (Oxford: Blackwell).

Strange, S. (1996), *The Retreat of the State: the Diffusion of Power in the World Economy* (Cambridge: Cambridge University Press).

Strange, S. (1998a), 'Globaloney?' *Review of International Political Economy*, 5 (4), Winter: 704–11.

Strange, S. (1998b), *Mad Money* (Manchester: Manchester University Press).

Stopford, J. and Susan Strange (1991), *Rival States, Rival Firms: Competition for World Market Shares* (Cambridge: Cambridge University Press).

Suranyi, G. (1998), 'Restructuring the Banking Sector in Hungary'. The Vienna Institute of International Economic Studies. Paper prepared for the 25th Anniversary Conference, 11–13 November, Manuscript number 18.

Török, A. (2000), 'Turbulences and Emergency Landings in Leased Planes: Macroeconomic Stabilization and Financial Sector Reform in Hungary in the 1990s', in Jens Holscher (ed.), *Financial Turbulence and Capital Markets in Transforming Countries* (New York: St. Martin's Press – now Palgrave Macmillan).

Tsoukalis, L. (1997), *The New European Economy Revisited* (Oxford: Oxford University Press).

US Department of Commerce (1999), *Hungary Investment Climate Statement, US Department of Commerce – National Trade Data Bank* (Washington DC).

Vernon, Raymond (1966), 'International Investments and International Trade in the Product Cycle', *Quarterly Journal of Economics*, 80 (May): 190–207.

Vernon, R. (1971), *Sovereignty at Bay: the Multinational Spread of US Enterprises* (New York: Basic Books).

Vernon, R. (1979), 'The Product Cycle Hypothesis in a New International Environment', *Oxford Bulletin of Economics and Statistics*, November, 41 (4): 255–67.

Vernon, R. (1993), *Sovereignty at Bay: Twenty Years After* (New York: St. Martin's Press).

Wallace, H. and W. Wallace (eds) (2000), *Policymaking in the European Union* (Oxford: Oxford University Press).

Wallace, H. and Alasdair Young (eds) (1997), *Participation and Policy Making in the European Union* (Oxford: Oxford University Press).

Wallerstein, I. (1989), *The Modern World System* (New York: Academic Press).

Wessels, W. and Simon Bulmer (1987), *The European Council: Decision-Making in European Politics* (Basingstoke: Macmillan – now Palgrave Macmillan).

Williamson, O. E. (1975), *Markets and Hierarchies: Analysis and Antitrust Implications: a Study in the Economics of Internal Organization* (New York: Free Press).

Tilles, S. (1963), 'How to Evaluate Corporate Strategy', *Harvard Business Review*, 1963.

Yoffie, D. B. (ed.) (1993), *Beyond Free Trade: Firms and Governments in Global Competition* (Boston: Harvard Business School Press).

Yuan, J. and Lorraine Eden (1992), 'Export Processing Zones in Asia', *Asian Survey*, 32 (11): 1026–46.

Zaszlasvsky, V. (1994), *The Neo-Stalinist State: Class, Ethnicity, and Consensus in Soviet Society* (New York: M. E. Sharpe).

Index